GUIDE

Vol 41 / Part 2
May 2025

Edited by **Rachel Tranter** and **Olivia Warburton**

7	**1 Corinthians** Helen Miller	*5–18 May*
23	**Numbers: discipleship in the desert** Helen Paynter	*19 May–1 June*
39	**God and female imagery in the Old Testament** Johannes J. Knecht	*2–8 June*
47	**James: faith-works as God's new community** Tim Welch	*9–15 June*
55	**Acts 1—9** Steve Walton	*16 June–6 July*
77	**Lamentations** Victoria Omotoso	*7–13 July*
85	**War and peace** Valerie Hobbs	*14–27 July*
101	**Hosea** Miriam Bier Hinksman	*28 July–3 August*
109	**Teachable moments:** **discipling on the way in Luke's gospel** George Wieland	*4–17 August*
124	**A disabled reading of the healing miracles** Tanya Marlow	*18–31 August*

BRF Ministries
15 The Chambers, Vineyard
Abingdon OX14 3FE
brf.org.uk | 01865 319700

Bible Reading Fellowship is a charity (233280) and company limited by guarantee (301324), registered in England and Wales

EU Authorised Representative: Easy Access System Europe –
Mustamäe tee 50, 10621 Tallinn, Estonia, **gpsr.requests@easproject.com**

ISBN 978 1 80039 360 8
All rights reserved

This edition © Bible Reading Fellowship 2025
Cover image © Jakub/stock.adobe.com

Distributed in Australia by:
MediaCom Education Inc, PO Box 610, Unley, SA 5061
Tel: 1 800 811 311 | admin@mediacom.org.au

Distributed in New Zealand by:
Scripture Union Wholesale, PO Box 760, Wellington
Tel: 04 385 0421 | suwholesale@clear.net.nz

Acknowledgements
Scripture quotations marked with the following abbreviations are taken from the version shown. Where no abbreviation is given, the quotation is taken from the version stated in the contributor's introduction. NIV: the Holy Bible, New International Version (Anglicised edition) copyright © 1979, 1984, 2011 by Biblica. Used by permission of Hodder & Stoughton Publishers, a Hachette UK company. All rights reserved. 'NIV' is a registered trademark of Biblica. UK trademark number 1448790. NRSV: the New Revised Standard Version Updated Edition. Copyright © 2021 National Council of Churches of Christ in the United States of America. Used by permission. All rights reserved worldwide. NLT: the *Holy Bible*, New Living Translation, copyright © 1996, 2004, 2015 by Tyndale House Foundation. Used by permission of Tyndale House Publishers, Inc., Carol Stream, Illinois 60188. All rights reserved. NASB: New American Standard Bible®, Copyright © 1960, 1971, 1977, 1995, 2020 by The Lockman Foundation. All rights reserved.

Every effort has been made to trace and contact copyright owners for material used in this resource. We apologise for any inadvertent omissions or errors, and would ask those concerned to contact us so that full acknowledgement can be made in the future.

A catalogue record for this book is available from the British Library

Printed by Gutenburg Press, Tarxien, Malta

Suggestions for using *Guidelines*

Set aside a regular time and place, if possible, when and where you can read and pray undisturbed. Before you begin, take time to be still and, if you find it helpful, use the BRF Ministries prayer on page 6.

In *Guidelines*, the introductory section provides context for the passages or themes to be studied, while the units of comment can be used daily, weekly or whatever best fits your timetable. You will need a Bible (more than one if you want to compare different translations) as Bible passages are not included. Please don't be tempted to skip the Bible reading because you know the passage well. We will have utterly failed if we don't bring our readers into engagement with the word of God. At the end of each week is a 'Guidelines' section, offering further thoughts about, or practical application of, what you have been studying.

Occasionally, you may read something in *Guidelines* that you find particularly challenging, even uncomfortable. This is inevitable in a series of notes which draws on a wide spectrum of contributors and doesn't believe in ducking difficult issues. Indeed, we believe that *Guidelines* readers much prefer thought-provoking material to a bland diet that only confirms what they already think.

If you do disagree with a contributor, you may find it helpful to go through these three steps. First, think about why you feel uncomfortable. Perhaps this is an idea that is new to you, or you are not happy about the way something has been expressed. Or there may be something more substantial – you may feel that the writer is guilty of sweeping generalisation, factual error, or theological or ethical misjudgement. Second, pray that God would use this disagreement to teach you more about his word and about yourself. Third, have a deeper read about the issue. There are further reading suggestions at the end of each writer's block of notes. And then, do feel free to write to the contributor or the editor of *Guidelines*. We welcome communication, by email, phone or letter, as it enables us to discover what has been useful, challenging or infuriating for our readers. We don't always promise to change things, but we will always listen and think about your ideas, complaints or suggestions. Thank you!

To send feedback, please email **enquiries@brf.org.uk**, phone **+44 (0)1865 319700** or write to the address shown opposite.

Writers in this issue

Helen Miller is head of research and professional development at Moorlands College and lectures on the College's MA and BA Applied Theology programmes. Helen and her husband Tim are involved in their local church in preaching and sung worship.

Helen Paynter is a Baptist minister in Bristol and serves as tutor in biblical studies at the Bristol Baptist College. She is the founding director of the Centre for the Study of Bible and Violence. She is the author of a number of articles and books, including, most recently, *Blessed are the Peacemakers*.

Johannes J. Knecht (PhD, University of St Andrews) is a lecturer in theology at WTC Theology and specialises in church history and systematic theology. His primary interests are patristics, Christology and trinitarian theology.

Tim Welch is the director of ministerial formation at Bristol Baptist College and tutor in practical theology. He lives in Cheltenham, where he also helps lead Hesters Way Baptist Church in his spare time.

Steve Walton is professor of New Testament at Trinity College, Bristol. He is a retired international volleyball referee and lives in Loughborough with his wife Ali, an Anglican minister, and their Border Terrier, Flora.

Victoria Omotoso is an honorary research fellow at the University of Exeter and a visiting lecturer at Sarum College and London School of Theology. Victoria is a writer, speaker and preacher, and is also the curator of *The Shalom Collective*, an online space to encourage people through God's word.

Valerie Hobbs is a linguist at Sheffield University and author of *An Introduction to Religious Language* and *No Love in War: A story of Christian nationalism*. In her spare time, she enjoys writing about the Bible.

Miriam Bier Hinksman is a Church of England curate in the Canterbury diocese. She has written *Perhaps There Is Hope* (Bloomsbury, 2015) and *Reading Hosea: A beginner's guide* (Grove, 2023).

George Wieland is a research fellow at Carey Baptist College, New Zealand, where he formerly taught New Testament and Mission. Prior to that, he and his wife Jo were involved in church and community ministry in Brazil and the UK.

Tanya Marlow is a writer, speaker and occasional pastoral theology lecturer. She specialises in biblical narrative and honest theologies of disability and suffering. Her books include *Those Who Wait*, and you can download her first book for free at **TanyaMarlow.com**.

The editors write...

Welcome to this new edition of *Guidelines*! There is plenty of challenge and tough thinking on offer in this issue, so we hope that you will approach the readings and reflections ready for God to speak into your mind and heart.

We cover a lot of both the Old and New Testaments in this issue. In the New Testament, we start with 1 Corinthians, where we are confronted with Paul's forceful, firm, yet kind letter to a troubled church. Our recurring three-week series begins with Steve Walton, who reflects on Acts 1—9. Tim Welch takes us through the brief but challenging letter of James, that infamous 'gospel of straw'. Tim helps us to see the pithy wisdom teaching, as well as the breadth of sayings and everyday illustrations that prove accessible and memorable for any age and culture.

We tackle some difficult Old Testament books in this issue. Helen Paynter takes us through the book of Numbers, often maligned as boring or irrelevant, and shows us how it crackles with excitement and depth. Victoria Omotoso helps us examine the book of Lamentations. She argues that the book is a form of protest, as well as a tool for processing the messy emotions of grief, anger and ultimately hope. Finally, Miriam Bier Hinksman guides us through Hosea, another book dealing with complicated emotions and sensitive issues.

George Wieland uses the gospel of Luke to accompany him as he identifies 'teachable moments' for both the disciples and for us today. Tanya Marlow also spends time in the gospels looking specifically at the healing miracles from a disability perspective. Johannes J. Knecht looks at six female images for God in the Old Testament, and explores the fact that scripture applies both male and female creaturely pictures to elucidate something of the beauty of God.

Perhaps the most challenging reflections come from Valerie Hobbs, who examines the theme of war and peace as she exposes the absurdity of war and its roots in greed and arrogance. She highlights the grief and restlessness that all earthly empires inflict, in tension with the hope for peace and justice God offers us both today and in the life to come. This series is deliberately provocative – I wonder what God will say to you through it?

Blessings,

Rachel   *Olivia*

The prayer of BRF Ministries

Faithful God,
thank you for growing BRF Ministries
from small beginnings
into the worldwide family it is today.
We rejoice as young and old
discover you through your word
and grow daily in faith and love.
Keep us humble in your service,
ambitious for your glory
and open to new opportunities.
For your name's sake.
Amen.

Helping to pay it forward

As part of our Living Faith ministry, we're raising funds to give away copies of Bible reading notes and other resources to those who aren't able to access them any other way, working with food banks and chaplaincy services, in prisons, hospitals and care homes.

'This very generous gift will be hugely appreciated, and truly bless each recipient... Bless you for your kindness.'

'We would like to send our enormous thanks to all involved. Your generosity will have a significant impact and will help us to continue to provide support to local people in crisis, and for this we cannot thank you enough.'

If you've enjoyed and benefited from our resources, would you consider paying it forward to enable others to do so too?

Make a gift at **brf.org.uk/donate**

1 Corinthians

Helen Miller

Attention to genre is important. We would have a strange view of the world if we couldn't distinguish the genre of newspaper from science fiction novel, for example. 1 Corinthians is a letter. Moreover, it isn't the first letter that Paul wrote to the church in Corinth. As a lecturer of mine liked to say, there is a zero Corinthians! We know this from 1 Corinthians 5:9–10, where Paul brings correction to a misunderstanding regarding his previous letter: 'I wrote to you in my letter not to… not at all meaning…' (When we are misconstrued by others, we can take heart that even Paul, with his eloquent precision, was – and no doubt continues to be – misunderstood by his readers, including ourselves!)

As we read on, we realise that we've entered a conversation. Paul has written to the church, and they have written back (7:1). Why is this important? Scripture speaks into all eras, but it is written within certain contexts. Attention to these contexts aids interpretation. The context of letters is particularly specific. Paul is writing at a particular time to a particular group of people who have particular questions and issues within their community. He knows about some of these through their letter. Their letter, however, hasn't shared the worst of what's going on. He knows about the divisions, for instance, through 'some from Chloe's household' (1:11). It is likely that these people have also told Paul about other issues he addresses.

As we go through 1 Corinthians, we'll therefore pay attention to what has prompted Paul's at times forceful response. I hope that we'll be both challenged and encouraged by Paul's kind but firm words to a troubled church.

Unless otherwise stated, Bible quotations are taken from the NIV.

5–18 May

5–11 May

1 Pointing forwards

1 Corinthians 1:1–9

In addressing chapter 1, it is tempting to dive straight into the main content (1:10–31). The opening section may appear as simply requisite formalities – the ancient equivalent of 'I hope this letter finds you well' before beginning what we really want to talk about. Alternatively, we might think that Paul is trying to find something nice to say before his extensive critique. Paul, however, does not waste words. These opening lines introduce the main themes of his letter. Here are some examples.

'Paul, called to be an apostle of Christ Jesus by the will of God' (v. 1). This is a standard opening line from Paul, although, interestingly, he refers to himself only as a servant when writing to the churches in Philippi and Thessalonica. Paul's letters to those churches reveal a healthier picture than 1 Corinthians. There are occasional warnings but, overall, Paul's encouragement is to persevere. In contrast, the Corinthian church has serious problems, one of which is a challenge to Paul's authority. In 1 Corinthians 4, therefore, Paul needs to reaffirm his authority while, simultaneously, redefining what authority looks like. It is fitting, therefore, that Paul reminds them here that he wasn't self-appointed, but sent by God as an apostle of Christ.

'To those sanctified in Christ Jesus and called to be his holy people' (v. 2). Paul's approach to moral living can be summed up by the phrase, 'Become who you are.' Paul addresses much unholy behaviour in 1 Corinthians. Here, however, he reminds the Corinthians that they have been cleansed and made holy through Jesus' work, not their own. They are called to walk in line with their new identity.

The second part of this verse is also noteworthy: 'together with all those everywhere who call on the name of our Lord Jesus Christ' (v. 2). Elsewhere in 1 Corinthians, Paul draws the Corinthians back to shared doctrine about Jesus: 'For I received from the Lord what I also passed on to you' (11:23; compare 15:3). The Corinthians are not to amend the truths that they have inherited and are called to pass on. Paul reminds them, therefore, that they're not an isolated group who can believe what they want but are part of a wider family.

As you read through the rest of these opening verses, look for other examples of where Paul points forwards to issues that he'll address in his letter.

2 The wisdom of the Spirit

1 Corinthians 2:6–16

The flow of Paul's argument is difficult to discern in chapters 1—4. How, for instance, does this section on the Spirit relate to division? Attention to other biblical texts and knowledge of Corinth's cultural backdrop sheds light on Paul's connection. Acts 18:24–28 introduces us to Apollos, who is described as a 'learned' man or, as the NRSV puts it, 'eloquent'. Aided by his eloquence, he 'vigorously refuted his Jewish opponents in public debate' (Acts 18:28). Acts 19:1 reveals that Apollos spent time in Corinth after Paul had planted the church there. In the ancient world, eloquence was prized. People would gather around the Sophists, itinerant philosophers, and associate themselves with the most impressive rhetoricians. In contrast to Apollos, Paul notes, 'When I came to you, I did not come with eloquence' (2:1). It is therefore likely that some in the Corinthian church were aligning themselves with Apollos over Paul because of Apollos' superior rhetorical skills. It is worth noting that some scholars think that there are two groups in Corinth, not four, and that Paul adds Peter and Jesus to exaggerate the issue and so highlight the ridiculousness of the division (1:12).

Paul is brilliant at getting to the root of an issue, rather than just addressing the symptom. He discerns that the Corinthians are looking for the wrong thing in their leaders: human impressiveness, rather than the power and wisdom that only the Spirit brings. In bringing correction, Paul argues that God's wisdom can only be communicated through the Spirit. As he's noted already, this wisdom is demonstrated most powerfully and counter-intuitively in Jesus' crucifixion. Jesus' death, Paul argues, is 'a stumbling block to Jews and foolishness to Gentiles, but to those whom God has called, both Jews and Greeks, Christ the power of God and the wisdom of God' (1:23–24). Therefore, the Spirit is not only needed to communicate God's wisdom, but also to receive it (v. 14). Only a mind illuminated by the Spirit can understand the things of God. Paul finishes with an astonishing claim, that such a person has the mind of Christ (v. 16b).

Let us pray that God will fill our minds with his Spirit that we would grasp the profundity of his wisdom and might – wisdom that is often counter-intuitive to our own ways of seeing the world.

3 True spirituality

1 Corinthians 3:1–23

The Spirit's centrality is still in focus as we turn to Paul's rebuke at the start of chapter 3. The 2011 NIV translation says, 'Brothers and sisters, I could not address you as *people who live by the Spirit* but as people who are still worldly' (v. 1a, italics mine). The NRSV translation differs slightly, 'I could not speak to you as *spiritual people*' (italics mine). 'Spiritual people' is a more literal translation of the Greek (*pneumatikos*). Paul certainly understands 'spiritual people' to be those living by the Spirit. In addition, the NRSV's translation better highlights the sting of Paul's rebuke. The Corinthians thought that they were spiritual! The problem is that their understanding of spirituality was distorted. As we'll see in chapters 12—14, the Corinthians associated spirituality with the more obviously supernatural gifts, particularly speaking in tongues (14:1–5). Paul affirms the blessing that speaking in tongues brings to the believer (14:14–18) but challenges the misuse of this gift in gathered worship. He lays the foundation for this challenge in chapter 3 by emphasising that true spirituality is not demonstrated in gifting or impressive speech, but faithful service to Christ.

Paul uses mundane (even, for the Corinthians, distasteful) metaphors to illustrate the nature of faithful service. Manual work was looked down on in the Roman world. Therefore, Paul's use of building and farming metaphors to describe his and Apollos' work seems deliberately designed to cut through his readers' pretensions. Through these analogies, Paul conveys that the distinguishing marks of a Spirit-filled servant are dependence on God (v. 7) and rootedness in Christ (v. 11). Only service characterised in these ways bears fruit that will last (vv. 12–14).

Petty division has no place in a Spirit-filled, Jesus-serving community (vv. 3–4). To illustrate this point, Paul makes a profound claim. The community of Jesus' followers are the new temple (vv. 16–17). Through Jesus' work, it is now within the Christian community, not a building's inner sanctums, that God's presence is encountered in its fullest tangibility. Paul's reference to division here demonstrates that he has not strayed from his original topic (1:10–17) but is continuing to unearth root causes. The Corinthians misunderstand both what true wisdom consists of and what receiving the Spirit looks like. May Paul's correction challenge us to seek the same humble service that he demonstrates and that characterises true spirituality.

4 United with Christ

1 Corinthians 6:12–20

Paul starts a new section in 1 Corinthians 5:1. In chapters 1—4 he rebukes the Corinthian church for their division over leaders (1:10–17). In chapters 5—6 we see that, ironically, although they divide over the wrong things, they're not prepared to divide over the right things! 1 Corinthians 5:1–12 reveals that they have tolerated a kind of sexual immorality that even the pagan Romans would not tolerate, 'a man is sleeping with his father's wife' (5:1). The most likely scenario is that he is sleeping with his stepmother after his father's death, perhaps to keep her wealth in the family. This man, Paul argues, should be expelled from the church until he repents, which is what Paul means by handing him over to Satan (5:5).

This passage raises the question of church discipline today. Examples we've seen or experienced of graceless heavy-handedness can cause us to avoid this topic altogether. However, Paul's arguments challenge those in church leadership to think carefully and compassionately about circumstances under which individuals may need to be excluded from some or all church activities for the safety of others alongside the church's witness.

1 Corinthians 6:1–8 provides further examples of the Corinthians dividing over the wrong things. Here Paul rebukes them for taking each other to court over 'trivial' matters (6:2), probably relating to property and money. The Roman civil courts were stacked in favour of the rich. Richer members may therefore be extorting poorer members through an unjust legal system.

The bleakness of the church's condition continues in verses 12–20 where Paul rebukes those who are sleeping with prostitutes. Paul highlights the abhorrent incongruity of those who are united to Christ uniting themselves with a prostitute. This argument pre-empts his more extended description of the church as Christ's body in chapter 12 – believers are 'members (or parts) of Christ' (6:15). Union with Christ is attained through Jesus' death and resurrection. Our old selves are crucified with Christ and we are raised with him as a new creation (Romans 6:1–14). This union is realised through Christ's Spirit within us (6:19). These truths are profound, but they are manifest in day-to-day living. Sexual immorality is not, in Paul's eyes, simply a bad thing to do in some abstract sense, but a denial of believers' new identity in Christ and a violation of his presence in their lives.

5 Citizens of heaven living on earth

1 Corinthians 7

This is a challenging passage. At first glance, for example, Paul's exhortation that 'those who have wives should live as if they do not' (v. 29) appears to contradict his earlier instructions on sexual intimacy in marriage (vv. 1–5). In addition, it is disputed whether Paul elevates singleness over marriage or presents both as equally valid paths. This passage's complexities illustrate why context is important when interpreting biblical texts. The context of the Corinthian church and this passage's location in scripture's wider story are important for ascertaining Paul's meaning.

In terms of the Corinthian church, I noted in the introduction that in 1 Corinthians we're entering a dialogue. Paul has written to the Corinthians, they have written back, and he is writing again, both in response to concerns raised by 'some from Chloe's household' (1:11) and to respond to their letter. Here Paul is responding to their letter (v. 1). He addresses their claim that men should not have sexual relations with women (v. 2). Why did they hold this view? One possibility is that the Corinthians have misunderstood Paul's previous letter and assumed that his prohibitions on sexual relations extend to marriage. Paul's correction affirms an equality in marriage that was countercultural to the norms of his day, with both husbands and wives called to yield their rights to each other (vv. 2–5). Paul's promotion of singleness was also countercultural. One emperor, for instance, issued legal penalties to women who didn't marry quickly enough following widowhood.

This passage's context in scripture's whole story is also important. Paul affirms the goodness of creation, including marriage. However, believers' lives this side of Jesus' return are relativised by the hope that awaits. 1 Corinthians 15 reveals that such eschatological expectation is lacking in the Corinthian church, which is why Paul employs such strong rhetoric here (vv. 29–31). As Gordon Fee explains, for Paul, 'one lives in the world just as the rest — married, sorrowing, rejoicing, buying, making use of it — but none of these determines one's life. Those who follow (as disciples of) the risen Christ are marked by eternity; therefore, they are not under the dominating power of the circumstances or conditions that dictate the existence of others' (Gordon Fee, *The First Epistle to the Corinthians*, Eerdmans, 2014, p.376).

In other words, Paul reminds the Corinthians that they are citizens of heaven, living on earth.

6 Reframing rights and apostleship

1 Corinthians 9

At first glance, 1 Corinthians 9 looks tangential to Paul's instructions about eating food sacrificed to idols (chapters 8 and 10). In addition, Paul appears to contradict himself, seemingly taking a stricter stance on this issue in chapter 10 than 8. This apparent discrepancy results from Paul's distinction between eating food sacrificed to idols and participating in idol worship. Some Corinthians, however, struggled to see this distinction. Therefore, those who eat food sacrificed to idols with a clear conscience should refrain from doing so for the sake of their brother and sister, who may otherwise be led astray. Once we recognise that Paul's instructions regard laying down one's rights for others, we see that chapter 9 is no tangential aside but forms the heart of Paul's argument.

In 1 Corinthians 9 Paul presents himself as an example to follow (see also 10:31—11:1). As the church's founder, he has the right to financial support (vv. 4–14). He has, however, not made use of this right but supports himself so that he can preach 'free of charge' (v. 18). He has also adapted to the cultural context of those he is seeking to reach, laying down his right to his own preferences to present the gospel as winsomely as possible (vv. 19–23).

However, although laying down rights is Paul's key point in chapter 9, he has a secondary argument too. Paul's refusal to take financial support from the Corinthians may be one of the reasons that some are questioning his authority (v. 3). Given the issues in the Corinthian church, it is possible that Paul won't take financial support because he doesn't want to place the Corinthian church in the position of being his benefactor, or patron. Doing so may have made it harder for Paul to assert his authority over the church since, in wider Roman society, the one receiving support is expected to honour their supporter. Therefore, Paul's argument is not just that the Corinthians should lay down their rights as he has laid down his, but that his refusal to accept financial support proves, not undermines, his apostleship. It highlights his commitment to the hallmark of apostleship: a resolute focus on the good news of Jesus Christ and a desire to make this known as widely as possible.

Guidelines

If we are concerned about issues in our churches, 1 Corinthians reminds us that problems in church life are nothing new. In fact, hopefully the churches that we're part of are healthier than the church in Corinth! It is encouraging, therefore, that Paul has far from given up on the Corinthian church. His rebukes are firm. However, they stem from his love for the church and his concern that they live in accordance with their new identity as God's holy people (1:2) – that they become who they are.

We've seen Paul address various issues in the chapters that we've looked at so far: division (chapters 1—4), sexual immorality (chapters 5—6), legal wranglings (chapter 6), marriage and singleness (chapter 7), and the eating of food sacrificed to idols (chapters 8—10). All these issues relate to the Corinthian Christians' failure to realign their thoughts and actions in light of the gospel of Jesus. Paul's rebukes and instructions go beyond surface issues to the heart of the matter. He longs for every aspect of their lives to be reformed by the good news of Jesus.

As you reflect on the chapters that we've looked at so far, consider the following questions:

- Which of the issues that Paul has addressed are most pertinent for your own local church context?
- How does Paul address these issues? In particular, which aspects of the gospel does he bring to his readers' attention? What can we learn from this for our churches today?

1 Addressing attire

1 Corinthians 11:1–16

Much is disputed and unclear in this passage. Some things, however, are clear. Women and men are contributing to gathered worship. Paul doesn't discourage this. Rather, his concerns regard appropriate attire (or possibly hairstyles).

It is also clear that Paul is countercultural in his attitude towards women. The Roman world was patriarchal – although it was also economically hierarchical, so a rich woman was higher up the social strata than a poor man. It was a given in Roman culture that a man was head of the household (thus it is striking that Paul refers to 'Chloe's household' in 1:11). Paul's qualification of this headship in reference to Christ's relationship to his church and God's relationship to Christ is notable (v. 3). As Paul expands on in Ephesians 5:25, the power imbalance in Roman culture was not something husbands should abuse. Rather, following Christ's example, they were called to sacrificial love.

There is also agreement that the key issue here relates to honour. Wives dishonoured their husbands if they did not cover their heads or, some argue, if they wore their hair loose (v. 5). The Greek can be read both ways, although the stronger consensus is that hair coverings are in view here. Why might some women not be covering their heads? Elsewhere Paul rebukes divisions caused by wealth discrepancies (11:22). It is possible, therefore, that the wealthier women don't want to veil their heads because they have expensive hairstyles. An uncovered head in first-century Roman culture suggested availability and therefore, Paul argues, refusal to wear a covering brings shame on their husbands.

Paul's instructions relate not just to women, however. Men are not to cover their heads. Why would this be an issue? Men (and women) covered their heads when making an offering to the various gods and goddesses worshipped in Roman temples. It is likely, therefore, that Paul's instruction is to ensure that worship of Jesus looks distinctive.

Hair coverings for both men and women don't have the same meaning in much of contemporary Britain as they did in Paul's day. Nevertheless, his instructions remind us that attire is important. If what we wear is a distraction or stumbling block to others, Paul would urge us to lay down our right to wear what we want so that we can be a blessing to others.

2 Discerning Christ's body

1 Corinthians 11:17–34

The Words of Institution in verses 23–26 are perhaps so familiar that we overlook their original context. That context is far removed from the sombre ceremony that constitutes the Lord's Supper in many churches today. The picture Paul paints is of an unruly party, within which 'one person remains hungry and another gets drunk' (v. 21). Paul rebukes the Corinthians not because they celebrate the Lord's Supper within a shared meal. This was common practice in the early church (e.g. Acts 2:46). Paul's complaint is that their shared meals look more like pagan banquets than Christian fellowship around the Lord's table.

It is difficult to ascertain what is going on at these shared meals. Paul indicates that the believers are divided by wealth (v. 22). This may be because richer members are arriving earlier than poorer members and consuming the best food and drink before they arrive. More probably, the richer members are sitting on couches around the table with the poorer members at the peripheries. In 1 Corinthians 12 Paul indicates the countercultural equality that comes through believers' sharing in Christ's body – as we'll look at in tomorrow's notes, Paul flips the Corinthians' pre-established hierarchies on their head. Paul is therefore incredulous that an act remembering their Saviour's death could be celebrated in a way that shames poorer members.

Paul's response is to direct the Corinthians to the centre-point of their faith: Christ, the Passover Lamb, who gave his life for us that we might have life in him. 1 Corinthians 15 reveals that, alongside failing to understand Jesus' death, at least some of the Corinthians disbelieve in his resurrection. Here, Paul reminds the Corinthians that the Lord's Supper points back to Christ's death and forward to his return (v. 26). Paul warns the church that their desecration of the Lord's table is bringing God's judgement upon them. He calls them to discern the body of Christ before they eat and drink. What does it mean to discern Christ's body? The language of Christ's body is applied both to the Eucharistic bread (10:16; 11:24) and the church (12:12–31). Which is in view here? Probably both. By shaming and excluding the poorer members, the Corinthians are undermining the power and profundity of Jesus' sacrificial death. Paul exhorts them to discern, or to recognise, both the significance of Jesus' sacrifice and their unity as his body.

3 Unity in Christ

1 Corinthians 12:12–31

Paul wasn't the first to use the body as a metaphor to encourage unity. A Roman historian called Dionysius recounts a fable told by a Roman general in the fifth century BC to discourage agricultural workers from revolting against their rulers. In his fable, the general likened the workers to hands and feet and their rulers to a stomach. 'One day,' he narrated, 'the hands and feet got fed up. "We do all the work," they complained, "while the stomach does nothing but gets all the food."' They went on strike. 'What,' asked the general, 'was the result? The whole body died of starvation.' His fable was effective. The revolt was averted.

Comparing Paul's use of the body metaphor with others, including this fable, helps us understand his meaning. One central difference leads to others. The church is not just *a body, it is Christ's* body (12:27). In Ephesians and Colossians Paul describes Christ as the head of his body. Indeed, in Ephesians 5:21–33, Paul integrates his body metaphor with his analogy of the church as Christ's bride, emphasising the intimacy of believers' union with Christ. How do believers experience this union? Paul answers this in 1 Corinthians 6:12–20, where his use of the body metaphor (6:15) is followed by a description of believers as a temple of the Holy Spirit (6:19; see also 12:13). Christ is at work in and through believers' lives through his Spirit.

Christ's presence in his church impacts how unity is understood. As in the general's fable, usually the body metaphor was used to reinforce social hierarchies. If everyone sticks to their place, it was reasoned, society will function well. Never mind that some are doing all the work while others get all the food! The church is different. Paul challenges the Corinthians' hierarchies by arguing that it is not the respected who need to be honoured, but those who lack honour (v. 23). In addition, it is not the seemingly stronger parts who are indispensable, but those who seem weaker (v. 22). It is disputed whether the divisions that Paul addresses result from an over-elevation of certain gifts (particularly the gift of tongues) or wealth discrepancies or, more likely, both. Regardless of the cause, Paul's analogy reminds the Corinthians that their union with Jesus should radically transform their relationships with each other.

4 A pointed poem

1 Corinthians 13

Paul's ode to love is often heard at weddings. It is an appropriate passage for a marriage ceremony, but this isn't its original context. Rather, 1 Corinthians 13 is located between two passages about spiritual gifts. 1 Corinthians 12 addresses spiritual gifts through the metaphor of the church as Christ's body. In 1 Corinthians 14, Paul addresses issues within the church's gathered worship. This sandwich pattern to Paul's argument (spiritual gifts – love – spiritual gifts) is a common rhetorical strategy in Paul's writings, indeed scripture as a whole. It's called a chiasm. Within chiasms, the middle sheds light on the topics either side of it. By locating this passage in the middle of his discussion on spiritual gifts, Paul emphasises to the Corinthians that using their gifts with love is far more important than which gifts they've been given (12:31b—13:3). They are to use their gifts to build others up (14:19), not to bring honour and prestige to themselves.

When we hear Paul's poem in the context of a wedding, it is easy to miss how pointed it is. If we pay attention to the wider letter, we see that everything love is, the Corinthians aren't, and what love isn't, the Corinthians are! There is jealousy amongst the Corinthian church (3:3), but love does not envy (v. 4). Love is not proud and does not boast; the Corinthians are and do (5:2, 6). Love does not dishonour others (v. 4), but richer members humiliate poorer members at the Lord's Supper (11:22). Some take others to court over trivial matters (6:2), but love keeps no record of wrongs (v. 6).

It is challenging to reflect on what Paul might write to our own church communities. How are we demonstrating attitudes and behaviours that are contrary to love? Another challenge is to substitute our own name for 'love' and assess how we measure up. Can I say with integrity that Helen is patient, Helen is kind, Helen does not envy, Helen isn't self-seeking, and so on? Such an audit draws us to Christ, the embodiment of love, with whom we find not just forgiveness but power to change. As John writes in 1 John 4:19, 'We love because he first loved us.' Let us pray that we will know more of the magnitude of God's love, poured out in Christ, and be empowered by his Spirit to love him and others in return.

5 Order out of chaos

1 Corinthians 14:26–40

1 Corinthians 14:34 illustrates the importance of reading passages in their wider context. Out of context, 'Women should remain silent in the churches' sounds like an embargo on women speaking. However, Paul has already addressed women who pray aloud and prophesy in church gatherings, and the issue he highlights is attire (or hairstyles), not speech. In 14:34, therefore, it is a certain type of speech that Paul is objecting to.

Exactly what behaviour Paul addresses is disputed. Regardless, the central issue is that the women he's referring to are being disruptive. So too are two other groups who are also told to 'be silent' (*sigao* in Greek): those who speak in tongues when there is no interpretation, and the one who is prophesying when another starts to speak. The NIV makes this repetition harder to spot by using different phrases for each occasion: 'keep quiet' (v. 28), 'stop' (v. 30), and 'remain silent' (v. 34). The threefold repetition of 'be silent' in the NRSV better highlights the pattern.

A teacher repeatedly exhorting their class to 'be quiet' reveals the state of the class – it is noisy! Paul's repeated refrain suggests that the same is true of the Corinthian church. Paul's rebuke indicates that people are talking over the top of each other rather than listening (some in tongues and others in their usual language). His solution isn't to ban the use of spiritual gifts; on the contrary he tells them to 'be eager to prophesy' (v. 39) and thanks God for his own ability to pray and praise God in tongues (v. 18). Rather, he instructs them to do everything 'in a fitting and orderly way' (v. 40).

How this relates to our church context depends on the church. The context that Paul is writing into is chaotic. Therefore, his instructions don't justify the exclusion of children who aren't perfectly silent and still, for example. Moreover, Paul's emphasis is not on order for order's sake. Order is necessary so that believers are edified as they gather (vv. 5, 17). This brings us back to Paul's chief emphasis in his section on spiritual gifts: love. Do we use the gifts God has given us for our own benefit and to bring honour to ourselves, or to be a blessing to others and bring honour to God?

6 The foundation of faith

1 Corinthians 15:1–11

What is the heart of Christianity? Pause and reflect on this question before reading on.

In verse 3 Paul sums up the gospel's heart in just one sentence (albeit a long one!): 'For what I received I passed on to you as of first importance: that Christ died for our sins according to the Scriptures, that he was buried, that he was raised on the third day according to the Scriptures' (followed by a list of people who had met the risen Christ).

On the one hand, Paul's outline of the gospel's core is narrow and concise. The good news is that Jesus died for our sins and was raised back to life. This has been affirmed in history, Paul argues, through those who have met him. Most of these people, Paul notes, are still alive (v. 6). In other words, if you don't believe me, go and ask them! On the other hand, Paul's outline of the gospel is as rich and deep as the Bible's whole testimony. Jesus' death and resurrection is not unexplained. Rather, both Jesus' death and resurrection are 'according to the Scriptures'. This assertion resonates with Jesus' words after his resurrection as he walks alongside two disciples. They don't recognise him and, when they lament to a seeming stranger their distress at Jesus' death, Jesus' response is sharp and to the point: 'How foolish you are, and how slow to believe all that the prophets have spoken! Did not the Messiah have to suffer these things and then enter his glory?' (Luke 24:25–26).

We then read: 'And beginning with Moses and all the Prophets, he explained to them what was said in all the Scriptures concerning himself' (Luke 24:27).

It would be wonderful to have a record of what Jesus said. Presumably he explained that he was the one Isaiah spoke of, who 'took up our pain and bore our suffering' (Isaiah 53:4), 'was pierced for our transgressions' (v. 5), and yet 'will see the light of life and be satisfied' (v. 11). What other passages or themes do you think Paul has in mind and Jesus spoke of?

Paul moves on in 1 Corinthians 15 to the hope of Jesus' return (vv. 24–28). This is central to the gospel too.

Go back to the first question. What's your answer now? Reflect on how 1 Corinthians 15 deepens and sharpens our understanding of Christianity's central claims.

Guidelines

In some ways, first-century Corinth was very different from the UK today. Temples to various gods and goddesses dominated the skyline. The Roman empire tolerated polytheistic worship so long as it reinforced the emperor's authority. It was thought that the gods and goddesses would only bless the town if everyone honoured them. The Christians' refusal to worship them would have prompted suspicion, if not open hostility. Therefore, although Christians weren't facing systematic persecution when Paul writes 1 Corinthians, their allegiance to Christ led to exclusion from aspects of public life which were intertwined with local religion. There were temptations for Christians to compromise their allegiance to Jesus. We see this in the Corinthian church. For example, in the chapters that we've looked at this week, we've seen abuse of the Lord's Supper (chapter 11), disorder in gathered worship (chapters 12—14), and doctrinal errors (chapter 15).

In other ways, however, first-century Corinth has lots in common with the UK. Christians today also face pressures and temptations to compromise. Therefore, I encourage you to read (or listen) to the whole of 1 Corinthians and reflect on the following questions:

- Where are there points of connection between our context and the church in Corinth?
- What can we learn from Paul about how to address areas of sin and brokenness in our own lives and in our local church?
- Pray in response to what the Lord has laid on your heart after reflecting on the questions above.

'Therefore, my dear brothers and sisters, stand firm. Let nothing move you. Always give yourselves fully to the work of the Lord, because you know that your labour in the Lord is not in vain' (1 Corinthians 15:58). Amen.

FURTHER READING

Kenneth E. Bailey, *Paul Through Mediterranean Eyes* (SPCK, 2011).

Matthew R. Malcolm, *The World of 1 Corinthians: An annotated visual and literary source-commentary* (Authentic Media, 2012).

Helen Morris, 'The City as Foil (not Friend nor Foe): Conformity and Subversion in 1 Corinthians 12:12–31' in *The Urban World and the First Christians*, edited by Steve Walton, David W. J. Gill and Paul Trebilco, pp. 141–59 (Eerdmans, 2017).

Robert S. Nash, 1 Corinthians (SHBC) (Smyth & Helwys, 2009).

Janghoon Park, 'The Identity of Death in 1 Corinthians 15:20–28: Understanding the Cosmic and Forensic Dimensions of Death in Paul' in 신약연구, vol. 19, no. 1 (March 2020), pp. 194–232.

Andrew Wilson, 1 Corinthians For You (The Good Book Company, 2021).

Ben Witherington III, *Conflict and Community in Corinth: A socio-rhetorical commentary on 1 and 2 Corinthians* (Eerdmans: Carlisle, 1995).

Ben Witherington III, *A Week in the Life of Corinth* (IVP, 2012).

Numbers: discipleship in the desert

Helen Paynter

When I agreed in 2021 to write a commentary on the book of Numbers for Wipf and Stock's *Bible in God's World* series, I didn't know the book very well. I'd read it many times, of course, but not studied it. When I read it through again, this time with the commentary in mind, I couldn't suppress a wry chuckle. If the average Christian in the pew thinks that the Old Testament is violent or boring, Numbers could be said to tick both boxes!

Violent texts I'm used to thinking about, so while I haven't bottomed out my thoughts yet, I feel I'm starting to get a handle on them. I won't particularly focus on them in this set of readings, though. You can't do everything, and quite frankly Numbers has blown me away with the depth and scope of its relevance and liveliness for discipleship and ministry.

Liveliness? Yes, really. The book has been done a sad disservice by whoever chose to name it 'Numbers'. It sounds boring before you start reading it, and as the first couple of chapters read like the phone directory, readers could be excused for setting it aside for more pacey texts. Our Jewish brothers and sisters have been much wiser. They call the book *bəmidbar*, which means 'in the wilderness'. Now you're talking! Suddenly the book is fraught with peril, crackles with excitement and promises psychological depth.

And so it proves. But for those of us who read it as Christians, there is an extra blessing. Because if, as scripture clearly teaches, the Passover event is paralleled by the rescue of the cross, and if the settlement in the land of Canaan is a mirror to the eschatological rest of the saints, then the period in between reflects where we are now. Here we will see doubts and anxieties like our own. It is the mirror to the Christian life of discipleship. So – if it isn't too much of a mixed metaphor to say this about the desert – let's dive in.

Unless otherwise stated, Bible quotations are the author's own translation.

1 The thin Levite line

Numbers 1:47–54 3:14–39

We begin with one of those 'phone directory' passages that we tend to skim, or to skip altogether. But there is important theology here. If you have the time and inclination, pause and make a sketch of the arrangement of the camp, as described in these verses and in chapter 3.

What becomes clear when we do this is the double-ring arrangement of the tribes around the tabernacle. The twelve (which double-counts Joseph through his sons Manasseh and Ephraim, and excludes Levi) form a great ring 'some distance' (Numbers 2:2) from the sanctuary. Within that is a much thinner ring comprised of the Levites, by clan. Levi's sons Gerson, Merari and Kohath, now three clans, each cover one point of the compass. The east side of the tabernacle, where the entrance was (compare Exodus 38:13), is covered by Moses, Aaron, and their sons (Numbers 3:38).

What is the significance of this? A theme word in this passage is (*šmr*), which is translated in a range of ways, including 'care for', 'be in charge of', and in its nounal form, 'duty' (see, for example, Numbers 3:7–8). At its core, this word means 'guard', and this helps us understand the purpose of this double-ring arrangement. This protecting role is made explicit in 1:53: 'the Levites will camp around the tabernacle of the testimony, so there may be no anger upon the company of the sons of Israel'. They are to protect the people from the presence of the Lord, which is dangerous (compare Leviticus 10:1–2; Numbers 16:35). But they are also to guard the tabernacle itself (3:7–10, 38), especially from unauthorised intrusion (1:52; 3:10).

The physical arrangement of the camp, then, speaks of the unapproachable holiness of God, and to the priestly role of managing the encounter between humans and God without harm or desecration. This is also the place of mediation, where the intercessor makes a bridge between heaven and earth (cf. Numbers 8:19). We see Moses doing this in Exodus 32:9–12, 32; and Aaron doing it in an emergency situation in Numbers 16:46–48, in addition to the prescribed rituals (e.g. Numbers 15:22–31).

Ultimately it speaks of the great high priest who has made a permanent bridge between heaven and earth (e.g. Hebrews 4:14—5:7); and of our own role as a holy priesthood for the blessing of the world (1 Peter 2:5).

2 On jealousy and adultery

Numbers 5:11–31

We move directly from 'boring' to 'violent' – or at least, troubling. Read from the perspective of the 21st century, this is a difficult passage. Why is there no equivalent process to test the fidelity of a husband? What is going on with this ritual and curse? What is the nature of the punishment if the woman is found to be unfaithful? (Some have said miscarriage, but speaking from my perspective as a former doctor and now reader of Hebrew, I think a more plausible interpretation would be uterine prolapse or early menopause.)

But there are some important things to notice. First, despite the heading in the NRSV, it is not a passage 'concerning an unfaithful wife'. This is precisely wrong, since the ritual is designed to prove her faithfulness (v. 28). A better heading would be 'concerning a jealous husband' (compare v. 14). Nor is it a trial by ordeal, as many have alleged. That would require supernatural intervention to save her. (Think of the water and fire tests for witches in the Middle Ages.) By contrast, in this ritual the scales are tipped heavily on the woman's side. Unless there is divine intervention, the wife will be vindicated, and her husband's unfounded jealousy exposed publicly.

And, of course, male adultery is also explicitly forbidden (Exodus 20:14) and in ancient Israel adultery by man or woman punishable by stoning (Leviticus 20:10). In fact, it is one of the great puzzles of this text that it seems to ignore such a sanction if guilt is proved. This has led some to suggest that it is less about testing the virtue of individual women than proving the faithfulness (or otherwise) of Israel. Israel is, of course, often personified as a woman and wife in the Old Testament (e.g. Hosea 2:19).

But ultimately this passage reminds me of another woman brought to a holy man in accusation of adultery. And how he, like the priest in this passage (v. 17), also stoops to finger the dust. On that occasion, despite her evident guilt, she is met with the words, 'I do not condemn you. Go. And sin no more' (John 8:11).

3 Sheer devotion

Numbers 6:1–21

This may feel like (yet) an(other) obscure law from the distant past, but it has a surprising number of echoes in scripture. Samson was a (very bad) Nazirite (Judges 13:5), and so was Samuel (1 Samuel 1:11). It is likely that John the Baptist was, based on the angel's instruction (Luke 1:15) and on his likeness to the hairy Elijah. All of these were designated a lifelong Nazirite before their birth.

These examples are somewhat exceptional, however. Because what our verses in Numbers offer is essentially an instruction about a *voluntary* period of devotion. 'When a man or a woman vows a special vow, a Nazirite, to set themself apart for the Lord… in accordance with whatever vow they vow, so they shall do' (vv. 2, 21).

As Numbers sets it out, the period of dedication was also *temporary*. Its conclusion was marked with sacrifices and the cutting of the previously unshorn hair (vv.13–20). This seems to have been the pattern followed by the apostle Paul, who cut his hair in discharge of a vow he had made (Acts 18:18).

It might be chastening to any of us who have, unfairly, characterised Old Testament religion as law-bound and joyless, to understand that there were some men and women back then who chose to go well beyond the law's minimum requirements, as an act of pure devotion. Nor is there any transactional quality to this action. The devotee is not seeking to twist God's arm or blackmail him in some way. Sometimes we Christians use fasting in that way.

The circumstances that might lead to such a vow are not prescribed, which leaves it open for a range of situations. Gratitude, love, worship – we can imagine any of these might inspire such an action. Psalm 116 points to one example. 'I love! The Lord heard my cry for mercy, he turned his ear to me… What shall I return to the Lord for all his goodness to me? I will pay my vows to the Lord' (vv. 1–2, 12, 14).

It's inspiring, isn't it, this unbidden, agenda-free act of love? Like pouring perfume on the Master's feet, perhaps.

4 Bearing and setting the Name

Numbers 6:22–27

In 1979, a child helping out on an archaeological dig in the Hinnom Valley discovered a lower burial chamber that had been hidden from grave robbers by a rockfall. Among the many finds was a small silver scroll, hidden in a clay pot. It contained these words from the book of Numbers. Dating from the 7th century BC, it is the earliest fragment of scripture that we possess.

And what a beautiful piece of scripture it is! Its loving presentation in silver and its placement beside the body of a deceased loved one suggest that the ancient people of God thought so, too.

Although most modern translations use two different words for God's face in verses 25 and 26, the same Hebrew word is used for both. Here is a relatively unusual example of parallelism between two verses rather than within a verse (such as in Proverbs 1:28). Translated more literally, the two verses read:

May Yahweh cause his face to shine upon you, and may he be gracious to you.

May Yahweh lift up his face towards you and may he give you peace.

The 'face', that is the presence, of God is viewed as a source of great blessing. Compare this with Moses' words in Exodus 33:14–16, or the psalmist's in Psalm 139. In Psalm 80, the request for the radiant face of God forms a refrain in a song that longs for salvation.

What is the result of this presence? As the priestly blessing sets it out: grace (v. 25) and peace (v. 26). Grace to cover over the past, and peace for the future. It is surely no coincidence that the apostles sent greetings to their churches with these words (e.g. Romans 1:7; 1 Peter 1:2; 2 John 3).

In speaking these words, the priest would 'set the name of Yahweh' upon the people (v. 27). The idea of bearing the name of the Lord is one that runs through both testaments, and has to do with representing him to the world around (e.g. Acts 9:15). This is an awesome responsibility (cf. Exodus 20:7; Matthew 6:9), but it is a privilege that we must rise to: speaking blessing; being agents of grace and peace; and pointing people towards the radiant face of God.

5 Melons and garlic remembered

Exodus 16:1–5; Numbers 11:4–9

We know that memory and smell are closely related in our brains. We will all have experienced a sudden memory flashback triggered by a smell from our childhood. In Numbers 11 the people's boredom with manna (graciously provided by God, see Exodus 16) leads them to look back wistfully towards the food they ate in Egypt. In fact, their nostalgia gives us quite a detailed account of the menu they had in that country. As we hear the people reminiscing, we can almost imagine them salivating.

'Who will feed us meat? We remember the fish we used to eat in Egypt for nothing, the cucumbers, the melons, the leeks, the onions, and the garlic; but now our strength is dried up, and there is nothing at all but this manna to look at' (Numbers 11:4–6).

But they are quite wrong. They did not eat 'for nothing'. Their diet was calculated to allow them to continue to slave in the Pharaoh's brick factories. Their food was the only thing they received in lieu of wages.

What is it with the human temptation to look back on the past with rose-tinted spectacles? It's hardly conceivable, but these people only came out of Egypt a few weeks before. Have they forgotten the lash of the whip so soon? Have the calluses on their hands healed so quickly? Have the joys of freedom dissipated already?

Why can they not cry out to God in their hunger without casting longing eyes back upon an imagined history? Without constructing a false memory of plenty and ease? Without painting a whitewash over the past and projecting their desires upon it?

I am reminded of Psalm 73, where the troubles the psalmist is experiencing cause him to look with envy at those he calls 'the wicked' – the people who do not trouble themselves with attempting to walk in God's ways. Just as the psalmist is tempted to be envious of those who do not struggle with walking God's way, so the Israelites were tempted to look back with rose-tinted spectacles at the slavery that God had just saved them from. Maybe this is something we find connection with. Maybe the struggle sometimes feels too much.

For the psalmist, he realised how ludicrous that envy was when he entered the presence of the Lord and everything fell into perspective (v. 17). In the wilderness, where all else is stripped away, a fresh perspective can come to us.

6 Zelophehad redeemed

Numbers 27:1–11; 36:1–13

There are two purposes for the census in Numbers 26. First, it is a count of the fighting men (v. 2). But it is also conducted in preparation for the division of land after the conquest (vv. 52–56). And, of course, this is not just any old land; it's about perpetual inheritance in the promised land. It's about having a place among God's people forever.

But Zelophehad has died before the battle starts, and before the allocation of land begins. He is unable to stake his claim. He needs a kinsman-redeemer. The kinsman-redeemer is a close family member who acts on behalf of one who is unable to act on their own. He will purchase family property that has been sold (Leviticus 27:9–25), buy family members out of bonded servitude (Leviticus 25:47–55); and, like Boaz, preserve the family line (Ruth 4:5–6).

Whenever the technical term for kinsman-redeemer (*go'el*) is used, it is always a man who is in view. But Zelophehad has no sons (Numbers 26:33). So who will act on his behalf? Enter his daughters Mahlah, Noah, Hoglah, Milcah and Tirzah. This is a great disruptive moment. Zelophehad needs a *go'el*, and he gets five.

It's a story in three acts. Act One: the request. The women come forward, asking 'give to us a possession among our father's brothers' (Numbers 27:4). Moses has never heard this question before. So, quite rightly, he consults the Lord. And the word comes back, 'The daughters of Zelophehad are right' (v. 7). This is a redemptive move. And it gets written into the law. From now on, when a man dies without sons, his daughters can inherit.

But then comes Act Two: the pushback. In come the heavyweights, the heads of the ancestral houses (Numbers 36:1), to make a counter-appeal. If the women marry outside the tribe, the family land will be whittled away (vv. 3–4). It's unclear whether their request is motivated by self-interest or legitimate concern for their descendants. But, in essence, this landmark legal ruling is viewed as a threat. And so the provision is wound back a bit.

Act Three: the convenient memory lapse (Joshua 17:1–4). The land has been conquered and the victors are dividing the spoils. And, apparently, everyone has forgotten about the promise. The women have to make their appeal all over again. Two steps forwards, one step back.

19–25 May

Guidelines

If, as I suggested at the beginning of the week, the Israelites' time in the wilderness somehow mirrors our own discipleship, located between the resurrection and the eschaton, then the book of Numbers contains rich themes for meditation.

There is much to reflect on concerning our role as a royal priesthood, standing as it were between heaven and earth and called by God to represent him in the world. The New Testament's teaching of the priesthood of all believers, or, more properly, the priesthood of the church (rather than the individual priesthood of millions of individuals) invites us to lean into the Aaronic roles of blessing and intercession. And while, of course, atonement is the once-and-for-all and particular achievement of Jesus the one true Priest, the church is called to participate by helping people to step into its benefits.

There are also rich themes for meditation in terms of individual discipleship. The mistakes that Israel made are mistakes that we, too, are prone to: forgetfulness, ingratitude, faithlessness, grumbling. But we, like them, can be sustained by our daily bread, feasting not on manna but on the Bread of Life. And the faithfulness of God, his unwavering commitment to his promises, his steadfast love – these never change, and are worthy of our utmost devotion.

26 May–1 June

1 Mother Moses?

Numbers 11:10–17

Poor Moses! He never wanted the job in the first place, and tried hard to wriggle out of it when God first called him at the burning bush (Exodus 4:1, 10, 13). We join him here as the people are – not for the first time – moaning and grumbling. And – not for the first time – he is having an almighty strop with God.

Despite the will of God being written across the sky in fire and cloud, time and again the people prove intractable. It is after not one but two episodes (11:1–3, 4–10) where their moaning and groaning have displeased the Lord that Moses has this outburst. But let's pay closer attention to his language:

'Did I conceive all these people? Did I give birth to them, that you say to me, "Bear them in your lap like a nurse carries an unweaned child"… Where is meat for me to give to all these people? For they weep upon me saying "Give us meat that we may eat." I am not able to bear all these people on my own. For they are too burdensome for me' (vv. 12–14).

I'm struck by the feminine language here – the language of conceiving, birthing, suckling, feeding, comforting and carrying. Moses' complaint to God stems from the fact that he loves his people like a mother. In fact, perhaps he loves them too much. To him it doesn't feel as if they're all in it together as they journey through the desert. He feels as if he's carrying them like a mother carries a reluctant toddler.

His love is shown by his stubborn refusal to give up on the people. He has interceded on their behalf, even offering to bear that wrath on their behalf (Exodus 32:9–12, 32). He constantly positions himself between the people and the God they are constantly aggrieving (see also Numbers 12:13; 14:13–19; 16:22; 16:46). No wonder he is disintegrating under the weight of it all.

It interests me that his language of mothering, of bearing the people, is very similar to language that God uses of *Godself* in Exodus (19:4).

Has God really demanded all this of Moses? Or has he taken on too much – has he shouldered a burden that God would have carried? Indeed, has he himself missed the opportunity to be borne in God's arms?

2 Miriam's challenge

Numbers 12

The Cushites were a high-status warrior race (see Daniel J. Hays, 'From Every People and Nation: A biblical theology of race' in *Biblical Theology (NSBT)*, InterVarsity Press, 2003, pp. 87–103) and so, despite common modern assumptions that Miriam and Aaron despised Moses' wife on account of her dark skin, the siblings are probably complaining about Moses' *hubris* in marrying her. This fits with the next part of their complaint, 'Is it really only by Moses that the Lord speaks? Or does he not also speak through us?' (v. 2).

Many readers are troubled by apparent misogyny in this text. Why does Miriam alone receive punishment? It may help us if we notice that she is represented as the primary agent here. By the narrator's use of the feminine singular verb (literally, 'Miriam spoke, along with Aaron, against Moses'), her autonomy and leadership is highlighted. This has already been evident throughout her story; she has acted as a protector (Exodus 2:4–9); as a prophetess (15:20–21); and here as a moral agent.

Though we may feel discomfort at her being singled out for punishment, we should notice the unexpected leniency with which she is treated. Unlike Korah (Numbers 16), she does not die for challenging Moses' authority. Rather, following the appearance of her 'leprosy', she is put outside the camp to wait seven days to prove her healing. It is a transient phenomenon, and in the meantime the entire community of Israel waits for her (v. 15).

The description of her affliction is also noteworthy. Her leprous flesh is likened to the macerated corpse of a still-born child (v. 12). While male shepherds may have seen such a thing in livestock, a human foetus would probably have been disposed of by female birth attendants. Might a woman have had a hand in the writing of this narrative?

But it is most instructive to focus on the content of Miriam's challenge. In the previous chapter, Moses has expressed longing that all God's people might be prophets (Numbers 11:29). But Miriam has previously been described as a prophetess (Exodus 15:20–21). So when she asks the question, 'Does the Lord not also speak through us?', the answer is emphatically – yes! Stroppy as she is on this occasion, Miriam is the foremother of all the women through whom God has spoken since.

3 Asking the right questions

Numbers 13:1–20

The Israelites are on the cusp of the promised land. Nothing stands between them and the promise of God except their own resolve. (Not even the Jordan River – the route that Joshua takes a generation later is quite different.) As they gear up for what lies ahead, God instructs Moses to send twelve men into the land to check it out.

A key technique for reading Hebrew narrative is to spot repetitions (of a narrative, a speech, a set of instructions) and then pay attention to the differences. Doing this can be very fruitful for following the breadcrumbs that the narrator has left for us. Here, we have the repetition of the instructions for the scouts in God's words, and then Moses'. Let's compare them.

Yahweh's command concerning the twelve men is brief: 'Send men to reconnoitre the land of Canaan which I am giving to the people of Israel' (v. 2). But Moses' instructions to them far exceed this succinct instruction, amounting to a detailed surveillance operation.

'Go up there into the Negeb and then go up into the hill country. Look at the land – what is it like? The people dwelling in it – are they strong or weak? Are they few or many? And what is the land like that they inhabit? Is it good or bad? And what are the cities like that they inhabit? Are they in camps or fortifications? And what is the land like? Is it fertile or barren? Are there trees, or not? Take courage, and bring back some of the fruit of the land' (vv. 17–20).

Essentially, Moses instructs the scouts to report back on two things: the fruitfulness of the land and the achievability of taking it. He has no business asking either question. God has repeatedly told the people that it will be a land flowing with milk and honey (e.g. Exodus 3:8). And he has promised to give the land to them (e.g. Exodus 6:8). For this reason, I understand God's intention to be an investigation of *How?* – an expedition to determine strategy. But Moses' questions are *Can we?* and *Should we?* This is a feasibility project.

Herein lies the root of the people's fearful failure to enter the land (see chapter 14). Those who lead God's people must beware of propagating their own anxieties. Rather, we should set an example of faith.

4 Striking the rock

Numbers 20:1–13

Why is God displeased with Moses for striking the rock? Was it really such a grave sin that he had to be barred from entering the promised land (v. 12)? The full explanation for the prohibition probably lies beyond the events of this chapter, and we have touched on some of the other possible reasons in previous readings this week. But once again, it will benefit us to pay attention to what God commands, and what Moses actually does. God tells him to take the staff (v. 8), which he does (v. 9). God tells him and Aaron to assemble the people (v. 8), which they do (v. 10). But when God tells Moses to *speak to the rock* (v. 8), he speaks to *the people* and he *strikes* the rock (vv. 10–11).

Why is this such a big deal? Perhaps the clue lies in what Moses says. We might expect him to reproach the people for their lack of trust. *Oh faithless people, don't you know yet that God will provide for you?* But he says something quite different. 'Listen, you rebels, shall we bring water for you out of this rock?' (v. 10). There's a subtle but important difference. Moses doesn't seem exasperated at the people's lack of faith in God, but at the people's lack of faith in *him*. He doesn't represent the provision of water as a renewal of God's provision for his people, but as *his*, Moses', response to the people's request.

What has shifted in Moses to bring him to this dangerous conclusion?

Since he first came to them in Egypt, the people of Israel have held Moses responsible for all that is happening to them – especially when it's negative. It's all his fault, his responsibility. Here are some of the instances: Exodus 15:23–24; 16:2–3; 17:2; Numbers 14:2; 16:35–41.

Poor Moses has had the expectations of the people pressed upon him again and again and again. And somewhere along the way, he has come to believe the lie. The people are thirsty, and *his* honour is at stake. As we saw in an earlier reading, he is overwhelmed by the burden he thinks is his to carry.

Taking responsibility for the work that only God can do is both too great a weight to bear and too great a presumption to assume. It is a weight which will crush us. It is a presumption which will corrupt our souls.

5 The irrevocable word of God

Numbers 22:1–19

The presence of the Israelites in the region is, unsurprisingly, seen as a threat by some of the people-groups around. Here we see Balak, king of Moab, attempting a creative approach to what he perceives as a problem. Ultimately, his ploy hangs upon his belief that if the right person utters a curse over the Israelites, they truly will be cursed (v. 6). Balak, in common with most people in his day, believes that there is power in such utterances when they are accompanied by the relevant rituals. So he sends a deputation to Balaam, cash in hand (v. 7).

Tempted by the offer, Balaam promises to consult God for permission (v. 8). So far, so good. And God does indeed appear to him overnight, but not with the message Balaam was hoping for. 'Do not go with them; do not curse the people, for they are blessed' (v. 12).

When Balaam reports this to the messengers the next morning, he simply says, 'The Lord has refused to permit me to go with you' (v. 13). This betrays his lack of understanding. The project is not just forbidden (though clearly it is); it is fundamentally impossible. The people cannot be cursed, because *they are already blessed*. Balak thinks that whomever Balaam curses will be cursed, but the deeper reality is that whomever God has blessed is irrevocably blessed.

Ignorant of this deeper dynamic, the two parties separate. Balak's messengers return to him, and Balaam goes about his business, presumably congratulating himself on his obedience despite the temptation of hard cash.

But the temptation is about to be renewed. Informed simply that Balaam has refused (v.14), Balak naturally assumes that the man is hoping for a more lucrative bribe. So he sends even more distinguished envoys (v. 15), with an even better offer (vv. 17–18).

Now, if Balaam had truly understood the force of God's prohibition and the power of his blessing, he would have sent this second deputation back with a flea in their ear. And, initially, his words do sound pious. 'I am not able to transgress the command of the Lord my God' (v. 18). But he invites them to stay over, because 'I want to learn more of what the Lord will say to me' (v. 19).

Perhaps God's words are negotiable, or his blessing has reached its expiry date? No, Balaam; what God says cannot be unsaid. You have a lot to learn.

6 A truthful speaker

Numbers 22:20–35

Balaam was clearly a legend in his own lifetime. As we saw yesterday, he had an international reputation. He could command enormous speaking (or at least, cursing) fees. But as we began to discover, his grasp of the character of God is somewhat deficient. He has failed to appreciate that God's word is weighty, and it is a weighty thing to speak for the Living God. Rather, he is a sort of prophetic prostitute. If the price is high enough, his principles can be flexible. It hasn't been a very flattering portrait so far. Today things are going to get worse.

In response to Balaam's second appeal for permission to go to Balak, God has (reluctantly?) given permission (v. 20). This is perhaps an example of the common biblical trope of God giving people head to follow their own wicked inclinations (compare Exodus 4:21). But we might also notice that the permission is provisional: 'but only the word I speak to you shall you do' (v. 20). So Balaam is on his way – he thinks – to earn himself a small fortune.

Although the text doesn't label him as such, Balaam is clearly represented as a diviner – a seer, or a prophet. These are the people who had the power to invoke the sort of curse the Moabite king is after. So it is rather embarrassing, frankly, that Balaam utterly fails to notice the angel with the drawn sword standing in his path (v. 31). This is a portentous and dangerous phenomenon (compare Joshua 5:13–15; 1 Chronicles 21:16), and one that a man who claims to be conscious of spiritual realities might perhaps have noticed. Instead, he is bettered by his donkey, who proves to have more spiritual sensitivity (vv. 23, 25, 27), and can see what the seer cannot.

Here, as elsewhere in scripture (e.g. 2 Kings 6:14–23; also see Mark 8:22–25 in the context of the whole chapter), inability to see functions as a metaphor for spiritual blindness. But Balaam's humiliation is not complete until the donkey turns around and rebukes him (vv. 28–30). His beast has proven more spiritually sensitive, wise and truthful than him.

Balaam might have an international reputation and be able to command huge speaking fees, but as it turns out, God isn't impressed by such accolades. He can speak through anyone.

Guidelines

Studying this book has provoked me in many good ways, not least through the challenge it has offered in the consideration of my own ministry. I wouldn't have liked Moses' job: it was dangerous, difficult and pioneering in all the hardest senses of that word. The people were truculent and at times ungovernable. How can we lead well in such circumstances? And we should dare to ask the question: *Does* Moses lead well? There is surely much to commend him for. He loves, weeps for and prays for his people. He consistently and faithfully points them towards God and God's promises. But he is also anxious and gives the persistent impression that he feels the outcome rests on his shoulders rather than on God's.

In Numbers 11:16–25, we read of Moses' appointment of 70 elders to share his burden. In response, the Lord pours out his spirit upon them. 'And when the spirit rested upon them, they prophesied, but they did not again' (v. 25). *They do not prophesy again*. In fact, we read nothing further of these elders, ever again in the story. Did they fail to step up, shirking their share of the work? Were they just there for the glamour of the spiritual experience, and faded away when the real responsibility started? Or did Moses refuse to share the burden, when it actually came to it? Was he one of those leaders who complains about his workload but won't actually delegate anything to anyone else, because nobody else can do the job properly? Did he rather enjoy the feeling of being put-upon; the importance of being indispensable?

Maybe these were temptations for Moses. Maybe they are temptations for us.

Balaam teaches us that it is a high and holy calling to speak in the Lord's name. And Moses teaches us that it is a high and holy calling to lead the people of God.

FURTHER READING

Carmen Imes, *Bearing God's Name: Why Sinai still matters* (InterVarsity Press, 2019).

Helen Paynter, 'Who is the Wife Whose Virtue is Tested in Numbers 5?' in Helen Paynter and Peter Hatton (eds), *Attending to the Margins: Essays in honour of Stephen Finamore* (Regent's Park College, 2022).

Helen Paynter, 'Better to fall into the hands of God: a narrative and theological reading of Exodus 32' in *Journal for the Study of Bible and Violence*, forthcoming.

Jay Sklar, *Numbers (Story of God Bible Commentary)* (Zondervan Academic, 2023).

God and female imagery in the Old Testament

Johannes J. Knecht

Having grown up in church and absorbed the language used there to speak about God, one would almost be forgiven for thinking that God is masculine. The language we generally tend to use for God, on a superficial analysis at least, does give that impression. Theologically speaking, however, we would have to argue that God does not partake in, nor is he subject to, either sex or gender. As the one who is the complete other, God very clearly is neither male nor female, nor non-binary for that matter, as this still implies a certain meaningful relationship to the creaturely descriptor of sex or gender.

Nevertheless, since God has revealed himself to a created world, using human language, we cannot but acknowledge that God has chosen to use language and images to self-describe which are, in essence, often gendered. As good readers of scripture, we always ought to interpret and aim to understand those passages, without imparting the concept of the gender of the language, or the image used, into the nature and being of God.

Even though *most* images used for God in scripture are male (King, Father, Lion, Warrior, etc.), certainly not all are. This week, we will take some time to reflect on the passages in the Old Testament scriptures where God is described with female imagery. The aim will not be to show that God is female, or anything of the sort, but rather that scripture applies both male and female creaturely pictures to elucidate something of the beauty of God.

Unless otherwise stated, Bible quotations are taken from the NIV.

1 The calming mother

Psalm 131

So much said in only three verses. The psalmist encourages the reader or singer to be calm, to quietly know that God keeps them safe and sound. This psalm is internally connected to some other psalms surrounding it: Psalm 120 and 130, for instance. The encouragement, 'Israel, put your hope in the Lord', clearly aims to show that Psalm 131 is speaking alongside and with Psalm 130 (compare Psalm 130:7). In this encouragement lies a deep truth: God can be trusted, and this trustworthiness should allow us to rest assured.

The psalmist juxtaposes some sources of stress in verse 1 with the source of calm and quietness in verse 2. The restlessness described in the first verse has to do with the pressure to achieve, to aim for, to occupy oneself with those things in life which are out of reach. Striving for things that, for whatever reason, are out of reach, is a deep internal source of stress and anxiety. If we live in such a way that we are busy to achieve the things that lie above us, that are out of reach, we are working in vain and will inevitably increase our levels of unrest. At the same time, if the psalmist were to think he was 'higher' placed than others, this would be a source of arrogance and self-reliance.

Verse 2 is the antidote to all of this. Like a child that is calm with her mother, so the psalmist is calm in the knowledge and assurance that God cares, that God is near, and that they are safe. If a young child wakes in the middle of the night and is upset, being with their mother almost always calms them. The psalmist uses this picture of intimacy between a mother and child to describe his own sense of calm and assurance. God is like a calming mother, in whose nearness we may feel secure.

2 The labouring mother

Isaiah 42:10–17

In this section of the book of Isaiah, God shows himself from a variety of different angles. The first three verses in the section (vv. 10–12) encourage the congregation to praise JHWH. In poetic language, the author describes all that the world has to offer: land, seas, islands/coastlines, cities and mountains: the call to recognise JHWH as Lord is universal. This Lord, this JHWH, is the mighty warrior, the one who overcomes those who stand against him. Verse 13 displays the power and strength of God, as the one who battles and wins over those who stand against him.

A similar display of strength, vigour and power follows in verse 14. While God was quiet and silent in ages past, she now steps into the limelight as a woman in labour. The silence and quiet mentioned in this verse should not be interpreted deistically, as if God stood aside and was unengaged with his world. No, the picture is rather that whilst God's presence and work was perhaps unnoticed before, it is impossible to miss now. In the same way that it is impossible to ignore the fact that a woman is in labour, when you are near, the work of God cannot be missed. There is nothing apathetic about the act of giving birth: it is all-encompassing, requires complete focus and attention. This is not saying that this work of God was in any way all-encompassing in relation to God's own nature, but it does paint a picture that God was fully engaged in what he was trying to achieve. Important to notice about this image of God as a woman in labour is that it occurs in first-person speech. She describes herself here, in God's own words, as a groaning, gasping and panting woman in labour: such a striking image.

The whole section (vv. 14–17) is probably about the return of the people of God (v. 16) and thus about their salvation from bondage. An interesting parallel can be seen with Isaiah 41:18–19, but here we also see the other side of that same salvific act: where it included flourishing of the desert in Isaiah 41, it means the drying up of the vegetation here. As God makes his works of salvation known as a woman in labour, loudly and clearly, he is seen to demonstrate both acts of judgement (vv. 15, 17) and loving care (v. 16).

3 The watchful mother

Isaiah 49

Accompanying the first of the servant songs (Isaiah 42) we saw the image of God as a mother, and now, again, in the second servant song, we see the image of God as a mother utilised to explain God's faithfulness and love for his people. The text contains some ambiguity as to who the Servant actually is. Language like 'from the body of my mother he named me' (v. 1) would suggest a certain individual, with whose history, family and beginnings God is intimately acquainted. However, verse 3 identifies the individual with Israel.

Verse 5 again brings up the 'womb' of the mother of the Servant; the place where the Lord formed the Servant with his task to 'bring Jacob back'. In other words, God knew the Servant's very beginnings and intended them to serve God in a particular manner. Hence, when we come to verse 15, it is the third time in this chapter alone that maternal language is used. Verse 14 introduces the third instantiation of maternal imagery, in response to Zion's exclamation of being forsaken and forgotten by the Lord. Zion assumes that the promises made to Jacob/Israel are not for her, but the following makes clear this is not the case. What goes for Israel, goes for Zion. Hence, verse 15 returns to the picture of God's motherly care, already applied twice in the Servant song, to counter Zion's worry: as a mother who is always aware of her child, especially when it is being fed of her own body, God could never forget or lack compassion for her child.

A mother forgetting her nursing child is presented as a rhetorical impossibility: it is the strongest image Isaiah can come up with to display God's dedication to her children. However, even though a mother's attention and care for her children is nigh impossible to break, God's care and attention for his people even exceeds a mother's (v. 15). The image of being inscribed on the palms of God's hands is a similar picture of God's condescension, his willingness to stoop low to be near. Normally, as a sign of belonging, the master would write his name on the hand of the servant in his household. God does it the other way around: we are written on his. Isaiah paints a beautiful picture of the Lord's deep dedication and love for his people, in this chapter exemplified by a mother's love for her child.

4 The peaceful mother

Isaiah 66:1–14

The beginning of this chapter sees a firm affirmation of God's sovereignty over creation. The majesty of God is such that heaven can be thought of as his seat and earth his footstool. Considering this awesomeness, what kind of human house can possibly and suitably be built for such a God? The rhetorical question is simply answered with a resounding: none. God is the origin of all that is: he has made it all. This text is reminiscent of the conversation between David and the Lord in 2 Samuel 7.

What follows in the next five verses is a litany of judgement, particularly the judgement of amalgamated or syncretistic worship. Even though the forms of worship (the offering of an ox, a lamb, grain, or frankincense) look biblical and trustworthy, the worshippers 'have chosen their own ways' (v. 3), probably meaning that they have strayed from the intended meaning and execution of those rituals. As such, they are worthless and sinful, akin to killing a person, offering pig's blood, or worshipping an idol. In verses 3 and 4, the self-centredness of the human sacrifices comes to the fore: they 'chose what displeases me' (v. 4). The sacrifices described do not place God at the heart of these rituals, but rather the worshippers themselves and, as such, God rejects them.

After verses 1–6, which mainly contain sentiments of judgement, the chapter returns to hope in verses 7–14. As in chapters 42 and 49 of the same book, the image of motherhood takes centre-stage once again, this time first in relation to Zion or Jerusalem and then, in verse 13, as God. Verses 7–9 reflect on the hopeful promise that the curse of a painful childbirth, given in Genesis 3:16, will at some point be overcome. A painless birth indeed can only be the result of God's involvement, God's wish to bring the people of Israel salvation. In both verses 10–11 and 12–13, the image of the mother is a comforting, calming presence. As such, the well-being of Jerusalem, and act of rejoicing over her, in the first pair of verses, is a source of great joy and comfort. Verses 12 and 13 similarly apply that image of motherhood to God: just as a mother brings peace to and comforts a child, so God will comfort his people, and they will be satisfied and content.

5 A proud mother

Hosea 11:1–11

This text is probably best known for its use in the New Testament to signal the prophecy that Jesus would be returning from a time in Egypt as a child. However, in the context of Hosea, God recounts the history of the Exodus, one of the most momentous events in the history of the people of Israel. God called his people to him, but they did not want him and decided to turn to other gods and deities. There is an intense sadness in those first couple of verses as God argues that his longing and the pulling away of the people of Israel are inversely correlated: the more God wanted to have them close, the more he called them to himself, the stronger the reaction of the people to pull away. It is an image very much at home in the story of Hosea.

Verses 3 and 4 show God as a caring mother who teaches the young child Ephraim how to take his first steps. Especially paired with the image of the Exodus in verse 1, which included 40 years of wandering on foot through the desert, the 'taking of the first steps' suggests that the time in the desert was a period in which God raised Israel up as a people, teaching them how to move and walk on their own. Verse 4 underlines God's care: as she lifts her child up and takes the pain away, the mother also stoops down to offer the child food, probably from her own breast. The imagery used here, in verses 3 and 4, evokes God as a maternal figure who, with a sense of pride, watches and guides her child to walk, helping them to deal with whatever is causing them pain, and feeding them from her own self.

The pain of Israel's rejection of God's self-giving becomes even greater if we let that image sit for a bit, but it also explains God's inability to let her children perish and fall by the wayside (vv. 8–9). Even though God is frustrated and angry with Israel's unwillingness to be faithful, as a mother she remains loyal, faithful and trustworthy.

6 The protective mother

Hosea 13:1–14

This section in the prophecy of Hosea starts with a strong judgement on the people of Israel. First, it describes the downward trajectory of the people Ephraim, who, although they were held in high regard at first, fell through their worship of idols. This habit of idol-worship increased over time (v. 2). As a result, God warns that they will see the results of their idolatrous behaviour: they will vanish like the mist and the dew, they will be blown away like chaff blown from a threshing floor (v. 3).

As was the case in Hosea 11, the Exodus plays an important role in the narrative of Hosea 13. The Lord refers to the time in Egypt and the fact that the salvation of the people of Israel can only properly be ascribed to him. God is their saviour and therefore should be acknowledged as their only Lord. Furthermore, God's care was not restricted to guiding and drawing the people out of Egypt but included his care for them in the wilderness and land of drought (v. 5). However, when God had fulfilled his promise to the people of Israel, giving them a land of milk and honey, their satisfaction in worldly needs led them to forgetting their indebtedness to the Lord: 'they forgot me' (v. 6).

Verses 7 and 8 contain images of a God who is deeply hurt by the rejection of the people to whom he has shown his loyalty. The animals mentioned (the lion, leopard and bear) are all ferocious animals, known to be deadly. The habitual ignoring of the God who saved them and has shown mercy to them leads to a dangerous situation. Besides the threatening pictures of the lion and the leopard stalking their prey, the image of a mother bear who has lost her cubs is notoriously alarming. In the previous readings we mainly saw caring and loving female images, but now we see God described as a mother bear who has lost her cubs. Instead of calm and security, this image is meant to instil fear: a mother bear acting to protect her cubs is one to shy away from. Although geared towards Ephraim in this passage, the idea that this mother bear would similarly act to protect us as her children is, however, perhaps oddly comforting.

2–8 June

Guidelines

- Female images to describe the nature and being of God are rarer than their masculine counterparts, but they are unavoidable. How do you relate to these images?
- Arising from the biblical text and from theological reasoning, referring to God as 'she' might be warranted, as it could mean a mere accommodation of human language to describe a God who is neither male nor female, who does not partake in human descriptors like sex and gender. Would you be comfortable referring to God, under these parameters, as 'she' or not, and why?
- Are there other ways in which we might be importing creaturely descriptions into the being and nature of God? How could this become problematic, and how can we resist it?
- How do you think it is helpful to have these female images of God in scripture?

FURTHER READING

Lucy Peppiatt, *Women and Worship at Corinth* (Cascade Books, 2015).

James: faith-works as God's new community

Tim Welch

The letter of James takes around 10–12 minutes to read in its entirety, and yet we are not to be fooled by the brevity. Here is a collection of pithy wisdom teaching, covering a breadth of sayings and everyday illustrations that prove accessible and memorable for any age and culture. However, the reception of this letter has been sharply contested over the centuries, including the most famous rebuttal by Martin Luther who regarded James as 'an epistle of straw'. Herein exists the inherent tension within the letter, namely to what extent James' concentration upon works is the antithesis of the apostle Paul's major doctrinal emphasis on justification by faith (see 2:24). As we will note, several clues within the letter suggest that James assumes no separation between doctrine and praxis. Good deeds are the fruit of faith; hence these five chapters are regarded as the eminently practical outworking of true faith in God.

That said, James' letter provides far more than individualistic challenges for personal discipleship. James hits key issues that involve following Jesus together, as God's new community. In our readings we will consider the discipleship implications of contextual socio-economic inequalities wherever the church exists. Therein James urges readers to live out their faith brightly and counterculturally, with a practical wisdom that is from above (1:5, 3:17). Consequently, the personal and corporate goal is a maturing process whereby we may 'be complete and whole, lacking in nothing' (1:4). In this regard, surely James and Paul would agree!

While James restricts mention of the Spirit to one verse (4:5), the meaning of which is unclear, we can safely assume that the Holy Spirit's help is assumed to help Christians live out the implications of this brief epistle. For the real challenge with James is not the interpretation of the text, but the actual *doing*!

Unless otherwise stated, Bible quotations are taken from the NRSV. Author references are to works in the 'further reading list' on page 54.

1 Joy in trials

James 1

James dives straight in. He is first and foremost 'a servant of God and of the Lord Jesus Christ' (v. 1). Whatever other ministry credentials James might have added, perhaps as brother of Jesus or the leader of the church in Jerusalem as some reckon, the all-important status for James is that primarily he is a servant of God. For writer and readers, this same posture as God's willing and obedient slaves is to be emulated.

Such servanthood is also pertinent to the main thrust of chapter 1, that discipleship must be worked out in real-life contexts where troubles are to be expected as the norm. This has prompted some scholars (such as Moo, p. 25) to assume the letter should be dated in the mid-40s or 50s of the first century, when Jewish Christians were suffering regular famine, heightened injustices and increasing political hostility and danger. While pressing troubles will resonate with many contemporary global readers of James, it forces the question whether our own discipleship curricula assumes 'various trials' and includes the advice from James to 'consider it all joy' when responding to such painful realities.

Generally, we don't go seeking out trials, but soon enough tough challenges are likely to come our way. It's not a case of *if*, but *when*. Here, James links suffering to the process of maturity in the life of a believer, which opens deep mysteries of lived theology. How we respond to painful trials is, in James' estimation, an opportunity to flex our faith-muscles by persevering. After all, pain is the gift no one wants, yet in God's economy a secret supply of divine resources is promised: the generous gift of God's wisdom (v. 5) and the assurance of God's final crowning commendation (v. 12). The caveat James includes here, that we are to believe and not doubt (v. 6), has caused much consternation if it assumes an absolute and resolute belief. Thankfully, the context of chapter 1 recognises our human propensity to listen and then to quickly forget God's word. But as servants of God, we must listen, ask God for wisdom and then hold our nerve, as this should lead to action and maturity.

2 The 'partiality' faith test

James 2

Favouritism is a subtle temptation with insidious power. I remember the dynamic when an internationally known celebrity walked into our church and joined us for a few months. The buzz, the quiet whispers – 'look who is sitting over there', 'see their diamond ring' and the question 'why are their sunglasses kept on throughout the service?'. A few rows away sat another person, desperately poor, struggling to emerge from addiction and finding their way selling newspapers on the high street. As a church, whether we liked it or not, we were being presented with the James 2 'partiality' test, concerning what we really believe about others; and what is going on, motivationally, within ourselves.

James makes the contrast between 'pure' religion evidenced by practical mercy to widows and orphans (1:26–27), and the sinful discrimination of showing favouritism to the wealthy (vv. 1–13). God's bias is always to the poor and lowly, demonstrated supremely in Christ's incarnational poverty and the kingdom requirement to be 'poor in the world' (v. 5). Such theological truths are to have a bearing on Christian practice. Consequently, the impact of saving faith must be reflected in the new kingdom life as God's new community.

So this chapter acts as mirror and spotlight to penetrate the depths of our human heart. While celebrating the salvific nature of faith in Christ and the deliverance from the law that gives freedom (v. 12), James forces readers to conduct a self-examination to check there is not a gap between faith and works. In view of the examples James uses, it seems appropriate to check that discrimination and prejudice are not lurking deep behind our verbal statements of faith. He helpfully reminds us that salvation is not just a privatised spiritual or religious experience; rather, the implications are also to be corporate and holistic, involving clothes, hunger, shelter and meeting the needs of others (v. 16). How practical and how like Jesus (Matthew 25:34–45)!

With no dichotomy between a proclamatory and social gospel, the proof of true faith in the Lord Jesus Christ must always result in faith-works. With Old Testament examples of Abraham and Rahab to boot, James nails his point: 'You see that a person is justified by works and not by faith alone' (v. 24).

3 Oral care

James 3

The human tongue in an adult typically weighs around 50–60 grams. Visually, the tongue is not attractive to look at; yet this diminutive muscular organ in the mouth has the gigantic potential either for extensive good or for vast damage. With parallels found in the wisdom teaching of Proverbs, both 'death and life are in the power of the tongue' (Proverbs 18:21). Our words will ultimately reflect whether our wisdom is 'from above' or 'earthly, unspiritual, devilish' (James 3:15).

Here James starts this section with a sharp warning for any of us who are teachers or aspiring teachers (v. 1), probably aiming this missile at church leaders and teachers. Thereafter, he broadens out his challenge to all disciples of Jesus. After all, everyone faces similar struggles to tame and control their tongue. Although it is uncomfortable to dwell on the explicit reference to the responsibility teachers have for guarding their words more carefully, we note the pivotal role we each have. Whether we are leading churches, preaching, at home, teaching discipleship groups, leading children, running youth and family ministries, teaching in theological education or any other sector for that matter, our opportunity to influence others through our word output is massive. A contemporary application of James' point also challenges our use of social media, as online influencers or simply posting comments and opinions to those who follow us. James soberly reminds all that we will 'face stricter judgement' (v. 1).

Then, like a preacher using three illustrations, James ratchets up the challenge, showing how small things can have proportionately greater impact: think about the horse's bit, the ship's rudder and the spark that ignites a forest fire (vv. 3–6). Each example requires careful handling and control, otherwise the impact can be devastating. Similarly with the use of our tongue, which according to James is untameable (v. 7).

James thankfully includes realism that we all 'make many mistakes' (v. 2) with our words. He also amplifies Jesus' point, that 'what comes out of the mouth proceeds from the heart, and this is what defiles' (Matthew 15:18). So, when reading James 3:10–18, think about how the doctor asks us to stick out our tongue to assess our inner health. Let's seek true wisdom from God to enhance our spiritual health, with less duplicity of speech and more wise words of peace and righteousness.

4 War and peace

James 4:1–12

Having just accentuated the virtues of peacemaking at the end of chapter 3, James then asks the rhetorical question: where do conflicts and disputes originate (v. 1)? The reality of divisive church life in the first century was like the fragmented relationships in our contemporary church scene. So the militarist language James uses is striking and forceful (vv. 1–5), exploring the central issue about what constitutes the root causes for such bitter divisions among Christians.

While the typical human response in any conflict will often blame the other party, James places the fault squarely with us personally and the 'cravings' and self-desires that war within each of us (v. 1). Like a doctor's diagnosis, there is both bad news and good news to report here. The bad news is the problem hidden in the private realm of our inner attitudes, that if we harbour selfish and sinful attitudes to others, we are deemed guilty of murder. Jesus said the same in the sermon on the mount (Matthew 5:21–25). Alongside this stark diagnosis there is, however, a trace of good news which reminds readers that a supply of God's grace remains readily available within each conflict. Things could be solved by prayer, yet 'you do not have because you do not ask' (v. 2).

Here, James takes us back to our human predicament, that we so easily ask God with wrong or mixed motives, which have more to do with satisfying our agenda than God's reconciling purposes. Rather than regarding God as akin to a divine slot-machine, the encouragement here is for us to eliminate any spiritual adultery or double-mindedness (vv. 4, 8). While this section prompts honest self-inspection to ascertain if our inner desires are truly being brought openly to God, the pledge of 'all the more grace' (v. 6) offers tremendous hope and encouragement as the antidote to our human predicament.

In a battle zone there's no room for complacency or compromise. Similarly, the instructions in verses 7–12 add further encouragement that humility before God and others is not a passive spirituality; rather, it demands decisive action. Here, several explicit steps are listed for our attentive response, significantly centred around us taking the first step to 'draw near to God, and he will draw near to you' (v. 8). This seems an appropriate place for us to start today.

5 Wise wealth and time management

James 4:13—5:6

Planning is not negative or sinful. That said, the next topic on James' list of discipleship wisdom confronts the way followers of Jesus are prone to conduct business with flawed priorities. This links to the earlier stark warning, that 'friendship with the world is enmity with God' (4:4). James bluntly reminds readers of the insidious sin of presumption that can frame a day, month or year (v. 13) if we think we are in control of our own destiny. Although such planning may seem wise, if our plans fail to include God's perspective, we are exposed here as self-confident and self-deceptive. I remember a colleague regularly challenging us, 'Why do we as Christians so often live as functional atheists?', with a split between the sacred and secular spheres of our lives.

Herein lies an uncomfortable challenge, that making plans for our careers, promotions, housing, schooling, church, ministry – or whatever – should all be held lightly with the perspective that our life is like a 'mist that appears for a little while and then vanishes' (v. 14). While taking diary bookings and making commitments for months or a year ahead may boost self-identity and a need to be needed, James is on hand with two vital words that must always be remembered: *God willing!* ('if the Lord wishes', v. 15). This recognises our ultimate dependence when planning is always to be framed with humility, as we defer our agendas to God's will and purposes.

As a teenager, I remember how two letters were often uttered at the end of the church notices: 'D. V.' At the time I thought this was weird, and it was never explained; but later I discovered it was code for the Latin, *Deo Volente*, meaning 'God willing'. The intention was a right and proper recognition to comply with James' instructions that 'if the Lord wishes, we will live and do this or that' (v. 15). Just dropping the letters 'D. V.' in at the end of sentences implied 'D. V.' operated like a superstitious version of crossing your fingers or saying, 'Touch wood.' Instead, James here urges a much higher view of God from the outset, that truly embodies the wisdom Jesus taught about how to make plans and view wealth management for the genuine benefit of others in the cause of justice (5:1–6; and see Luke 12:16–21).

6 Patient, prayerful perseverance

James 5:7–20

These final and densely arranged verses of James' letter are directed to many Christians who were the recipients of the injustices against workers and harvesters just referenced (5:4). Like symmetrical bookends, James returns to his theme of fortifying God's people when experiencing trials of many kinds (1:2–3), with the clarion call for persevering patiently, even though they were suffering dreadfully (v. 10). In context, these are references to brutal realities experienced in everyday life, with no end in sight. Here James calls for a worldview that is possible only with the eyes of faith, namely, to await the imminent return of the Lord Jesus Christ (vv. 7–9) and to persevere in believing prayer (vv. 13–18).

This forces us to ask personal and searching questions of our own faith and discipleship, especially if or when we go through prolonged periods of personal suffering. James obviously decided some examples would bolster the case, so let's briefly consider the illustrations given for our personal application and eschatological hope:

1. The farmer – who is waiting for 'the precious crop from the earth, being patient with it until it receives the early and the late rains' (v. 7). As we endure trials, what fruit might God be cultivating in us and through us?
2. The Old Testament prophets – 'who spoke in the name of the Lord' (v. 10). Here's a challenge to remember those who have gone before us, who remained faithful to the end, while leaving final outcomes to God.
3. Job – famous for his patience in the face of devastating loss and affliction (v. 11). Job's honest struggles and questions eventually culminated in his final statement of faith: 'I had heard of you by the hearing of the ear, but now my eye sees you' (Job 42:5).

Job's example prompts James to challenge our use of words when going through trials, in a variety of contexts. These link the control of our tongue (3:1–12) with unequivocally truthful speech (v. 12), praying, singing (v. 13), confessing (v. 16) and expressing concern that goes after anyone who wanders from the truth (v. 19–20). Significantly, all these examples involve the impact of our personal speech within the relational life of our Christian community. That's how faith is to be worked out as God's new community.

Guidelines

The baseline for James' short letter suggests it is written by someone who has spent considerable time with Jesus, fully absorbing the teaching of the sermon on the mount (Matthew 5—7). As we have noted, James' direct punchy style relates to 'ordinary' experiences of everyday life, where personal theology and formation occurs. He makes the default assumption that recipients will face troubles; such are the realities of following Jesus then or now. The question is whether trials and suffering become stumbling blocks or stepping stones for growth and maturity of our faith.

Therein is a further angle in James' letter, that personal discipleship is never privatised solely for selfish gain. Our faith and holiness should always impact others with community benefit. Even the practicalities of our diary planning, using our assets and how we deal with conflict are to be translated into actions that benefit others, particularly the most vulnerable (1:27).

So, let's use this letter to enable a personal and practical spiritual health-check. In view of James' letter, reflect on the following aspects of your life and faith development:

- Draw three dials to depict the dashboard of your life – and indicate where you would gauge your recent (a) patience, (b) perseverance and (c) anger levels.
- Conduct a 'tongue' inspection – think about the quality of your words, and how you are speaking of others, privately and in public, for good or ill.
- Look at your diary and bank statements – where do they show your agenda blending with God's will and kingdom purposes?
- Think about prayers offered in faith (5:15) – how daring is your prayer life?

James reassures us that 'if any of you is lacking in wisdom, ask God, who gives to all generously and ungrudgingly, and it will be given you' (1:5). This enables the faith-works of God's new community.

FURTHER READING

J. Ayodeji Adewuya, *An African Commentary on the Letter of James: Global readings* (Cascade, Wipf and Stock, 2023).

Douglas Moo, *The Letter of James* (Eerdmans, Apollos, 2000).

Alec Motyer, *The Message of James: The tests of faith* (IVP, 1985).

Acts 1—9

Steve Walton

Luke tells the story of the beginnings of the church as the natural successor to his story of Jesus (notice echoes of Luke 1:1–4 in Acts 1:1). Luke wants to educate Theophilus, probably his sponsor in publishing his gospel and Acts, about not only what Jesus did on earth, but also what Jesus goes on to do – notice 'all that Jesus *began* to do and to teach' (Acts 1:1). So in reading this part of Acts, keep your eyes skinned for Jesus continuing to act in the story, as well as noticing language about God and the Holy Spirit acting. This book, in other words, is the Acts of God, rather than the apostles.

Yes, the apostles are important: the restoration of twelve following Judas' betrayal of Jesus is necessary (1:15–26), but once the Spirit falls at Pentecost, we rarely hear about most of the twelve. Peter is prominent in these chapters, and we're introduced to Paul, who will be very significant in Acts 13—28. But there's no evidence that the church grows through human planning and strategising: it happens in response to what God does.

Luke loves to provide previews of things to come, and you'll notice those as you read. For example, 2:38–39 models how someone becomes a believer: repentance, baptism in Jesus' name, forgiveness of sins, the gift of the Spirit and joining the believing community are all key features. Later conversion stories include most of these, although not necessarily in the same order. Look out for echoes of things like this in later stories, for such repetitions are Luke's way of telling us that these themes are important. They point us to ways that the narrative of Acts is being prescriptive for the church, and not just descriptive of what happened.

Unless otherwise stated, Bible quotations are taken from the NIV.

1 It's all about Jesus

Acts 1:1–11

Acts is Luke's volume two, and this section marks the transition between his gospel and this book. Volume one was about 'all that Jesus began to do and teach' (v. 1), which implies that Acts is about what Jesus continues to do and teach. The surprise is that he will no longer be present on earth, but he relocates to heaven (vv. 2, 9). So how can he act? Three features answer this key question.

First, Jesus will be active by the Holy Spirit, whom Jesus has taught them about (v. 4). The Spirit will baptise them (v. 5). The Spirit will empower them (v. 8). The Spirit is not Jesus' alter ego, a kind of Clark Kent to Jesus playing Superman – the Spirit is distinct from Jesus and serves the purpose of God by working on earth among people, and in Acts we shall see this happening regularly (see, e.g., 2:4; 4:8, 31; 6:10; 8: 29, 39).

Second, Jesus will be active through his disciples. They puzzle over his words about the Spirit's coming but know Jesus' mission involves restoring Israel to be all that she should be (v. 6). They aren't wrong to ask this question, for Jesus is restoring and renewing Israel as God's people – but to ask about its timing is an error (v. 7). So Jesus promises that they will be his witnesses (v. 8), which contrasts with Matthew's reporting Jesus' command to take the gospel out (Matthew 28:19–20). Gospel witness is both promised and commanded and can only be commanded because of the promised power of the Spirit for the disciples.

Third, Jesus himself will act from his place of authority at the Father's right side. His ascension into heaven (a phrase found three times in v. 11; NIV translates one as 'into the sky') places him in the throne-room of the universe. Human-centred and earth-centred geography need expansion to include this heavenly dimension of reality. In the rest of the book, Jesus will engage with the world by sending the Spirit (2:33), healing and doing remarkable things (3:6–7, 16; 4:10, 30; 8:5–8; 9:34), standing with his followers in danger (4:18–21; 5:19–20; 18:9), and even turning around the life of his arch-opponent, Saul (9:3–6, 17–22). Jesus is no absentee!

2 Reading scripture to interpret events

Acts 1:12–26

Jesus' followers knew they had to wait (1:4), and their proper instinct was to pray in unity while they did (v. 14). We see a group including women and men, totalling about 120 (vv. 14–15). During this transitional period, as they submitted to God in prayer, Peter highlights scripture to interpret the tragic story of Judas, the disciple who betrayed Jesus (v. 16). He draws on Psalms 69:25 and 109:8, two lament psalms concerning a godly person being betrayed at the hands of an ungodly person (v. 20): it's worth reading both psalms in full to see this. Peter lays these psalms alongside the story of Judas' gruesome death (vv. 18–19) to conclude that a replacement is needed.

Peter must have wondered how he himself was still there among the disciples, having betrayed Jesus himself (Luke 22:54–62). Jesus promised Peter that he would return after being 'sifted' by Satan (Luke 22:31–34), but Satan had 'entered' Judas (Luke 22:3). Both betrayals fall within God's sovereign purpose, for Jesus had to be betrayed (Luke 18:31–32; 22:21–22), and Jesus committed himself to upholding Peter. Peter stresses God's control of history by saying that scripture 'had to be fulfilled' (v. 16) and that it was necessary in God's purposes to replace Judas (v. 21).

So after Peter sets out the requirements (vv. 21–22), the group make a shortlist of two (v. 23). They then cast lots to choose one (v. 26). Some see this as an error and think they should have waited for Paul to come along, but that misses three things.

First, they pray to ask the Lord to make his will clear (vv. 24–25). Second, the purpose of casting lots is to put the decision into God's hands and out of human hands: 'The lot is cast into the lap, but its every decision is from the Lord' (Proverbs 16:33). This is not an unspiritual way of making a decision. It is not random chance, for God is sovereign. It is not that they should have waited until the Spirit came to guide them. Luke offers no criticism of their decision-making. The reassembly of the twelve by replacing Judas is vital to the restoration and renewal of the twelve tribes of Israel which Jesus is accomplishing through his followers. And third, Paul lacked the qualifications required, for he had not been a follower of Jesus during Jesus' lifetime (vv. 21–22).

3 The Spirit comes at Pentecost

Acts 2:1–21

In the first century, Jewish people longed for all God's people to experience the Spirit of God. Joel 2:28–32, which Peter quotes (vv. 17–21), is a prophetic promise of that day. Further back, in response to the comic scene of two of the elders being late to the tent of meeting, and yet prophesying in the Israelite camp as the Spirit fell, Moses expresses his desire that all God's people would have God's Spirit (Numbers 11:24–29). Pentecost represents the fulfilment of that longing, as the Spirit fills all the disciples (vv. 1–4). From now on, believers will be marked by experience of the Spirit, as Paul notes (Romans 8:9) – that's why it's puzzling when the Spirit doesn't fall on the Samaritan converts (8:16).

Three key features of this story help us understand this remarkable event. First, when God gave the torah to Moses at Sinai, there were similar phenomena: fire and loud noises, and God's close presence (Exodus 19:16–19; see vv. 19–20). Ezekiel looked forward to a day when God would write the torah on his people's hearts (Ezekiel 36:26–27), and the Spirit's coming is that day. Now God's will is no longer an external thing, written on papyrus, but it is internalised as the Spirit not only teaches disciples God's purposes, but also enables them to live in tune with God's will.

Second, Pentecost fulfils Jesus' promise that the disciples will receive the Father's promise of the Spirit (1:4–5), and that means that the time for witness to Jesus is here (1:8). The crowds hear their testimony to God's wonderful deeds (v. 11), probably what has been happening through Jesus, his ministry, death, resurrection and ascension. Their testimony is Spirit-empowered, and thus effective: some 3,000 people are baptised later that day (2:41).

Third, the Spirit's coming means that the 'last days' have begun (v. 17). Pentecost is a watershed in history, a change of the ages, so that the people of God now live in the final phase of world history before Jesus' return (1:11). Peter says nothing about how long this phase will last, but its characteristic is the ongoing activity of the Holy Spirit among the whole people of God, rather than only coming on specific people for specific tasks at specific times, such as Samson (Judges 14:19). In this new age, young and old, and women and men are included (vv. 17–18).

4 It's (still) all about Jesus

Acts 2:22–41

Peter now speaks at length about Jesus: this is the beginning of Jesus' disciples witnessing to him (1:8). Peter's testimony focuses on God's own testimony to Jesus. Thus God acted in and through Jesus' public ministry (v. 22), God's purposes were carried out in Jesus' death accomplished by the Jerusalemites and their leaders (v. 23), God raised Jesus from death (v. 24), God spoke in scripture to announce these events (vv. 25–31, 34–35), and God exalted Jesus to his right side and gave Jesus the Spirit to pour out (v. 33). It's vital for Peter's hearers to know that the God of Israel is active in and through Jesus, so that they respond to Jesus now, and are in tune with God's purposes (vv. 38–39).

In particular, Peter stresses the testimony of scripture to Jesus, quoting Psalms 16:8–11 (vv. 25–28) and 110:1 (vv. 34–35), interpreting them as pointing to Jesus as 'great David's greater son' because God raised Jesus from the dead. Peter reasons that David cannot be speaking about himself in Psalm 116, since his body did 'decay' (vv. 27, 29), and that David's 'Lord' cannot be himself (vv. 34–35; Psalm 110), and so he must be speaking of another Lord – Jesus, who sits at God's right side in heaven. He's not using scripture to prove Jesus' resurrection and ascension, but to explain and interpret them.

Further, and remarkably, Jesus now pours out the Spirit (v. 33). The Father has gifted the Spirit to Jesus after Jesus' exaltation to heaven, and Jesus has 'poured out what you now see and hear' – all the phenomena of sound and vision at Pentecost. In scripture and Jewish tradition, there is only one who gives the Spirit to humans, and that is God himself – and yet now the exalted Jesus is pouring the Spirit on his followers. Jesus is doing what God alone does, and that's why within a very short time the early Christians began to worship Jesus alongside the Father. Hence Peter concludes that God has declared Jesus to be Lord (that is, equal with God) as well as Messiah (v. 36). That's why people need to respond in repentant baptism as they call on Jesus, with the assurance that they will be forgiven, receive the Spirit and join this growing people of God (vv. 38–39).

5 Restoring Israel, restoring life

Acts 2:42—3:10

The renewed and restored Israel, recentred on Jesus, continues to grow as we learn here of its life and its reaching out beyond its bounds. Verses 42–47 are often (and rightly) read as a summary of the life of the earliest believers in Jerusalem, focused around gathering together to learn from the apostles, to share meals, and to pray (2:42). They met in the temple area (2:46): the phrasing indicates that their meals took place both in the temple and in homes: 'Day by day, spending much time together, they shared food with glad and sincere hearts both in the temple and by breaking bread in homes' (my translation; contrast NIV). In other words, their meals were public events, at least some of the time, following Jesus' example of welcoming 'sinners' to table (Luke 15:1–2; 7:37–39; 14:12–14). These meals, and 'overhearing' the apostles' teaching in the temple area, drew others to join the Jesus community (2:47).

In the mix of the community life, God did remarkable 'wonders and signs' through the apostles (2:43), and the next story goes on to give an example (3:1–10). The healing of the man with a congenital disability is not only a physical restoration, but also models and exemplifies the restoration Israel is experiencing. Notably, the first place the man goes after his healing is into the temple courts, praising God (3:8–9). This is the very place he has been unable to enter for more than 40 years (4:22). He moves (literally!) from being a passive recipient of charity at the temple gate to being an active worshipper within the temple area itself. He is now a fully restored Israelite who is no longer economically and physically dependent – indeed, he will be able to support others as he can now work. Like the public meals and public teaching, this public event invites Peter and John to speak to the rubbernecking crowds (3:9–10), and to invite them to become disciples too (3:11–26).

The disciples had asked whether Jesus was now going to restore Israel (1:6), and this section begins to offer an answer. Yes, Jesus is restoring Israel, and the restored Israel is becoming a community of sharing, of powerful deeds, and not of worldly power. The healing doesn't merely point to this restoration but is itself integral to the restoration process.

6 It's (yet again) all about Jesus

Acts 3:11—4:4

As in his Pentecost speech (2:14–36), Peter explains God's intervention in history. Here, Peter responds to the crowds who are amazed at the healing of the formerly disabled man (3:10–11). Peter is not now a man to miss an opportunity, by contrast with earlier denying that he knew Jesus (Luke 22:54–62). The Spirit's coming has changed Peter, and he's ready to speak about Jesus (3:13).

Like the Pentecost speech, Peter both centres on Jesus, and shows how God has acted in and through Jesus' life, death and resurrection. God – the ancestral God of Israel (3:13) – has glorified Jesus (3:13), raised Jesus (3:15, 26), speaks through Moses and the prophets (3:18, 21–25), and will send 'times of refreshing' (3:19) and ultimately Jesus himself at the time of restoring everything (3:20). All the way through, the initiative is God's.

The challenge to the hearers is what they will do with Jesus. He is the promised prophet like Moses (3:22; see Deuteronomy 18:15, 18) and, like Moses, his words are to be received obediently. We know there was a hope for such a prophet among the Qumran sect who wrote the Dead Sea Scrolls; they centred it on their Teacher of Righteousness, but Peter identifies Jesus as fulfilling this hope. Not only that, but Jesus also fulfils the whole storyline of scripture, back through the prophets, to the covenant God made with Moses, and right back to God's promise to Abraham that all the nations of earth will be blessed through his offspring (Genesis 12:3; 22:18; 26;4, echoed in 3:25). Here's a hint that God's purpose will embrace non-Jews; a key thread of Acts' storyline is how that comes about.

Given that this is who Jesus is, Peter states that Jesus' purpose is to bless these Jerusalemite Jews by enabling them to turn from their sin (3:26). As with God's action through Jesus, the initiative is God's, and people are now invited to respond. They and their leaders acted in ignorance (3:17), but there is a way back through repentance (3:19) – turning away from their ignorant sins back to God, so that they may experience the refreshing new life Jesus offers. In the beginning of a pattern found often in Acts, this call for repentance meets a mixed response – the Jewish leaders have Peter and John arrested (4:1–3), but 'many' who hear come to trust in Jesus through Peter (4:4).

16–22 June

Guidelines

We have noticed how focused the earliest Christians are on Jesus, especially in their teaching and proclamation of the gospel. In particular, at this time they stress the resurrection and ascension of Jesus to God's right side much more than Jesus' death (that will come later). Those events reverse the mistaken human verdict of crucifying Jesus (2:23; 3:13–14) and show the exalted status Jesus now has as 'Lord and Messiah' (2:36). Those events show that Jesus fulfils the scriptural hope for the true king of Israel who will eventually rule the whole world in God's name, and call people to turn from their own way of living to live under his rule (2:38; 3:26).

Jesus is now in heaven, at the Father's right side, the position of power and authority in creation, and he acts from there. The man with a congenital disability at the temple is healed 'in the name of Jesus Christ' (2:6, 16). Jesus pours out the Holy Spirit to empower and equip his disciples to live and proclaim the gospel (2:33; 1:8).

These themes together invite and incentivise us, as Christians today, to share our faith with others, for we know and experience Jesus in our own lives. We too have the Holy Spirit living in us individually and in our churches – the Spirit does not come to make us comfortable, but to call us out into mission (1:8). How might you and your church engage more fully in doing this in reliance on the Spirit's power?

Pray and think about this for some minutes, and jot down some 'first steps' from where you (and your church) are towards fuller involvement in God's mission to reconcile the universe with himself through Jesus and by the Spirit. Make them a matter of daily prayer for a week or two, and then consider what you might do and who you might share your thinking with.

1 Who speaks for God?

Acts 4:5–22

'How dare you claim to know what God wants!' That's a reaction Christians sometimes experience as we speak about Jesus and our faith in him. In some liberal, western settings there is tolerance except of claims to speak for God, since people either doubt there is a God at all, or doubt that anyone can know what God desires. This is an issue in this first court hearing of the apostles before the Sanhedrin, Judaism's highest court, and it will continue to be an issue in the next few stories in Jerusalem. Luke signals in several ways that Peter and John speak for God, and that the Sanhedrin do not.

First, Peter's speaking is empowered by the Holy Spirit (v. 8), and that means he speaks with a boldness and effectiveness which the Sanhedrin cannot gainsay (v. 13). Luke has told us in his gospel of Jesus' promise that the Spirit will equip the apostles to do exactly this (Luke 12:11–12).

Second, Peter's words focus on how God attests who Jesus is, by raising him from the dead, and by healing in his name (v. 10). More, it's only through Jesus' name that salvation is available (v. 12) – this is a big category which includes healing as well as God's transformation of people's status. Jesus is the cornerstone of God's purposes (v. 11, quoting Psalm 118:22).

Third, by contrast, the Sanhedrin don't even mention God in their questioning or their conferring alone. They are concerned only about how to suppress this new movement – and that in spite of the incontrovertible evidence of the man's healing (vv. 10, 14, 16). They are in danger of blaspheming against the Holy Spirit (Luke 12:10), for they order the apostles not to speak in Jesus' name (v. 18).

Fourth, Peter and John respond to the Sanhedrin's demand for them to be silent by focusing on the issue of what God wants (vv. 19–20). The apostolic band experience compulsion to speak about Jesus, a compulsion stemming from the Spirit's work (v. 8).

This confrontation is the first of others to come, both in Jerusalem and among Jewish people in the diaspora, the widespread community of Jews dotted throughout the Roman empire. It's about recognising the voice of God and then passing it on – if God has spoken and acted in Jesus, it would be arrogance indeed not to speak about it!

2 Spirit, prayer and power

Acts 4:23–37

When Jesus calls his disciples to pray at the Mount of Olives, they fall asleep (Luke 22:39–46). Here we see the close connection of the Spirit's coming, prayer and power for witness.

The Spirit's coming at Pentecost enlivens the company of believers so that now, when they have been instructed not to speak of Jesus (4:18), their first resort is to pray (vv. 23–30). This is the only substantial prayer recorded in Acts, so Luke clearly regards it as important. Notably, they pray to God as the 'sovereign Lord' who is creator (v. 24) – God holds the power and authority they need, and so they ask God for it.

Their prayer reads Psalm 2:1–2 (vv. 25–26) through the lens of recent events (vv. 27–28). Shockingly, they identify the opponents of God's work as including 'the peoples of Israel' (v. 27), whereas in the psalm they are the pagan nations opposed to Israel and her anointed king. Nevertheless, they are clear that God is in control of events – the death of Jesus was not merely a human act, but part of God's plan (v. 28).

So they ask with confidence for God to act by equipping them to speak boldly, and by healing and performing other remarkable signs and wonders in Jesus' name (vv. 29–30). They are not intimidated by the Sanhedrin's threats, but cry to God for power. That power comes, exactly as they ask (v. 31), not only at that moment, but in the continuing life of the believing community (vv. 32–37). The Spirit's power enables them to act and live with generosity of heart (vv. 32, 34–37) which fulfils God's purposes for his people in scripture (v. 34a echoes Deuteronomy 15:4). More people become disciples of Jesus through the apostles' testimony to the resurrection (v. 33). This vignette of the early Christians' communal life echoes that in 2:42–47, following the Spirit falling at Pentecost.

There's a cycle here: the Spirit's coming at Pentecost motivates and empowers them to pray aright; they pray for God to answer through the name of Jesus and by the Spirit; and the Spirit's power comes afresh to enable them to live and witness. The life of the Spirit, persistent prayer and power for living and witnessing are closely tied together – a church that has these is a church indwelt by Father, Son and Spirit.

3 Pain and gain: marks of God's true people

Acts 5:1–24

Following the glorious communal life of the disciples, verses 1–11 are a bucket of cold water, as is the arrest and imprisonment of the apostles (vv. 17–18). A further mark of a Spirit-empowered community is enduring pain and suffering – and that's what we see here.

Some pain comes from inside the community, as Ananias and Sapphira succumb to the corrosive power of greed. Rather than tell the truth – that they are giving part of the price they received for their property (vv. 1–4), they seek to appear more generous, and thus to gain social kudos like Barnabas (4:36–37). Alas, they are giving Satan space to operate within the community – this is not just lying but lying to God (v. 3). Luke is educating his readers about the kind of community Christians are: a community of generosity, truth-telling and open-heartedness. To act and think otherwise is to enter a place of great spiritual danger, for it violates the holiness of God's people, and of God himself. As often in Luke and Acts, how possessions are handled is an index of spirituality. Luke uses this scary incident to invite readers to examine their lives, to ensure that possessiveness is not dominant, and that their generosity mirrors God's generosity in Jesus.

Some pain comes from outside, as the Sanhedrin step up their campaign of persecution by arresting the whole apostolic band and imprisoning them (vv. 17–18). This would be easy to do as the Jesus followers met daily in the temple courts (v. 12). Nevertheless, God continues to answer the believers' prayer for boldness to speak (4:23–29) by sending an angel both to set them free and to tell them to keep speaking the life-giving gospel message back in the temple courts (v. 20: the original implies 'go on telling'; NIV has 'tell'). The comical scene of the temple police not being able to find them in the prison shows how out of tune with God the Sanhedrin are (vv. 22–24).

However, amidst the real and deep pain and suffering, God continues to work in answer to the church's prayer. The reputation of the community and the God they serve grows (vv. 11, 13). More people of both sexes come to believe (v. 14). God continues to work through his people to heal and deliver from unclean spirits (vv. 15–16), and the word spreads into the towns and villages of Judaea (v. 16). Yes, there's pain, but yes, there's gain!

23–29 June

4 Who is on the Lord's side?

Acts 5:25–42

This section picks up from the previous Sanhedrin hearing (4:5–22), which ended with the Jewish leaders telling Peter and John not to speak in Jesus' name. They echo that prohibition here (v. 28), but they are in a murderous mood by now (v. 33).

As in the previous hearing, the apostles respond to the accusation against them by focusing on God: they repeat that they must answer to God (v. 29; see 4:19–20). More than that, they focus on God in their response. Yes, the Sanhedrin are humanly responsible for Jesus' unjust death (v. 30), but Israel's God both raised Jesus from the dead (v. 30) and took him to his right side in heaven (v. 31). The Holy Spirit co-testifies with the apostles to these events (v. 32). Through this Jesus, repentance and forgiveness are available, even to the Sanhedrin who arranged Jesus' murder (v. 31). The apostles are superseding the Sanhedrin as God's spokesmen: the Council's murderous response shows they recognise this (v. 33).

So what about Gamaliel (vv. 34–39)? He is an elder statesman of the Sanhedrin, but he hedges his bets in his comments to the private session of the Council. He attempts to be neutral concerning the apostles and their message, and ironically speaks much truth: if the apostles' message and mission is God-given, the Sanhedrin will not be able to stop them (vv. 38–39). Indeed, Acts ends with the gospel proclaimed 'without hindrance' (28:31), which shows God is with the believers in their mission.

However, Gamaliel's attempted neutrality isn't achievable – you are either for or against Jesus the Messiah and his people, and Gamaliel's actions fail to support what God-in-Jesus is now doing through the Spirit in Jerusalem. Gamaliel and the Sanhedrin have the apostles flogged and order them not to speak in Jesus' name (v. 40) – these are not the actions of neutrality, but opposition to the gospel and its speakers.

The Sanhedrin attempt to dishonour the apostles, but the apostles understand that to suffer for Jesus is true honour (v. 41). It is following in the footsteps of the suffering Jesus, and Jesus himself said that suffering for his sake leads to blessing (v. 30; see Luke 6:22–23). The apostles continue to honour Jesus by announcing his Messiahship, thus fulfilling his promise that the gospel will spread (1:8).

5 How to handle community conflict

Acts 6

Don't let anyone tell you that the life of the earliest Christians was all sweetness and light! We've read of Ananias and Sapphira's lying and death (5:1—11), and here we see further conflict. Verses 1–7 reprise the theme of sharing among the believers, and transition to a focus on two of those chosen to resolve the conflict, Stephen (6:8—8:1) and Philip (8:4—40).

What's the argument all about? The Hellenists and Hebrews (v. 1) are groups marked by their predominant language. All are Jewish, but the Hellenists speak mainly Greek (the dominant language of the Jewish diaspora in the Roman empire) and the Hebrews mainly Aramaic (the dominant language of the land of Israel/Palestine at this time). Grave inscriptions in Jerusalem show that many diaspora Jews relocated to the land, especially toward the end of their lives, so that they could be buried there. Stephen is part of a Greek-speaking synagogue of such people (v. 9). The Greek-speaking widows, then, are probably women who moved to the land with their husbands, and the husbands later died. It's this group who believe they are being treated unfairly as the Jesus community shares food day by day (v. 1).

This is potentially a very damaging dispute, particularly because scripture emphasises that God's people must care for needy people, including widows, as a reflection of God's love for such people (e.g. Deuteronomy 10:18; 14:29; 24:17, 19–21; 26:12–13; 27:19; Psalm 68:5). The Jesus community's credibility in the eyes of their fellow-Jews is at stake here.

A community problem leads to a community gathering to resolve things (v. 2). Rather than representatives of the two groups negotiating, the twelve propose that a group of seven should set up arrangements to restore harmony (v. 3), so that the twelve may continue to focus on teaching and prayer (v. 4; recall the centrality of the apostles' teaching, 2:42). It's not that organising food is a lesser thing – both are called 'serving' (in verse 3 NIV has 'wait on', and in verse 4 'serving' – they're from the same word-group in the original).

The community solution leads to community growth (v. 7), because the community's reputation for justice is maintained, and the apostles keep testifying to Jesus. Stephen is a key part of that as he argues persuasively about Jesus among his fellow Greek-speakers (vv. 9–10). This gets him into trouble (vv. 12–14), but ultimately will lead to further gospel expansion (8:1–4).

6 Promises, promises!

Acts 7:1–16

Stephen's speech is the longest in Acts – what it says is important to Luke. Stephen appears before the Sanhedrin to face two charges: teaching that Jesus will destroy the temple and change Jewish customs understood to go back to Moses (6:14). Acts is clear that the accusers are speaking falsely (6:13), but these accusations require an answer.

Stephen responds by retelling Israel's history, picking out key figures from that story: Abraham and the patriarchs (vv. 2–8); Joseph and Jacob (vv. 9–16); Moses (vv. 17–43); and David and Solomon (vv. 44–50). The speech centres on the interplay between God acting and speaking, and human responses. Watch out for the way God is the subject of lots of the verbs – this is a God-centred reading of Israel's history. Look out, too, for the varied human responses to God: some demonstrate obedience to God, and some rejection of God and his messengers. You may find it helpful to skim-read Acts 7 identifying God's actions and words, and human responses.

This first part focuses on God's call to Abraham to migrate to the land (see Genesis 12:1–3). God is a promise-making God who assures Abraham of a new land, even though Abraham himself will not own any of it (vv. 3, 5). God's promise is made in Haran, outside the promised land (v. 2). Even though Abraham's people will live in Egypt, and there be enslaved and mistreated (v. 6), God promises they will be freed to worship in the land (v. 7).

It is in Egypt – again, outside the promised land – that God provides for his people in time of famine through Joseph (vv. 9–14). He is rejected by his brothers (v. 9), a pointer towards the Sanhedrin's rejection of Jesus (7:52). Here's a further theme of Stephen's speech: God is faithful to his promise to Abraham in spite of his people's rejection of the leaders he sends. God really can be trusted to carry out his promise and will ultimately do it in and through Jesus.

We're getting the first indications of Stephen's answer to his accusers. First, the temple is not now crucial to God's purposes in the light of Jesus' coming – indeed, God has always met people away from the promised land. Second, God is a promise-keeping God who cares for his people in spite of their rejection of his messengers, of whom Jesus is the most significant.

Guidelines

We've seen much of the earliest Christians' life together this week. Three marks of their community life are worth reflecting on for the life of our churches today.

First, they are dependent on God for the way they live. This appears in Peter's response to the Sanhedrin's question about how the man at the temple was healed, where the Spirit enables him to respond (4:8). It's clear from Peter and John's putting God first when told not to speak in Jesus' name (4:19). The community's prayer when Peter and John return shows that they need God's power and action to testify to Jesus (4:23–31). How does your church keep depending on God?

Second, they are dependent on one another in the way they live. Notice the sequence of events from the general description of sharing possessions (4:32–35), followed by the positive example of Barnabas (4:36–37), and the negative example of Ananias and Sapphira (5:1–11). This shows that social standing does not determine who gets resources in this community – rather, gifts are given by those who can (4:34) and distributed to those who need them (4:35). How does your church provide for people to give and receive?

Third, they handle conflict wisely and in a way which leads to growth rather than separation (6:1–7). This involves wise leadership, as the twelve present a possible response to the complaints of one group (6:2–4). It also requires a positive response from both parts of the community, seen in their nomination of seven who all have Greek names (6:5–6) – perhaps they are all from the complaining minority of 'Hellenists' (6:1). The delegation of responsibility to the seven leads to well-fed widows, demonstrating the reality of the believers' faith even to priests (6:7). How does your church deal with conflict?

1 God's rejected messenger, Moses

Acts 7:17–41

His accusers say Stephen claims that Jesus will 'change the customs Moses handed down to us' (6:14). This part of Stephen's speech shows how Moses fits into God's purposes, continues to relativise the role of the promised land and highlights how God's people reject God's messengers.

Stephen divides Moses' life into three 40-year segments: birth to 40 (vv. 20–28); 40 to 80 (vv. 29–34); and 80 to the time of God giving him the torah (vv. 35–41). Throughout, Moses is God's agent to free the Israelites from slavery in Egypt. He is prepared for this role by his upbringing in Pharaoh's household (vv. 21–22), and yet when he attempts to help his people, they reject him (vv. 26–27), and he flees to Midian (v. 29). God meets Moses at the burning bush and commissions him to lead God's rescue mission (vv. 34–35). Moses succeeds, and he receives the 'living words' of the torah on Mount Sinai (v. 38). Stephen makes clear that Moses is a divinely appointed leader, and that the torah is divinely given. Thus far, he agrees with his accusers about Moses and the law.

However, these events all take place outside the promised land. God meets Moses in Midian, the home of Israel's enemies who sold Joseph to Potiphar (Genesis 37:36), and who continued to oppress Israel (Judges 6:1–6). Indeed, the place in Midian is 'holy ground' (v. 33) – contrast the temple as 'this holy place' (6:13). Even the giving of the torah takes place in the Sinai Peninsula, in between Egypt and the land. God reveals himself away from both the temple's future location in Jerusalem, and even the land itself.

Although Stephen's accusers venerate Moses, the ancient Israelites reject him, not once, but twice: first, when he seeks to reconcile two of them (v. 26–27, 35); and second, by constructing and worshipping a golden calf at the very time Moses is receiving the torah (vv. 39–41). Stephen hints at the significance of Jesus by reminding the Sanhedrin of the 'prophet like Moses' to come (v. 37, quoting Deuteronomy 19:15). We have already heard Peter speaking of this prophet, and how dangerous it is to fail to obey that prophet's words (3:22–23). The Sanhedrin need to pay heed, lest they also reject Jesus, the prophet like Moses, in their day. The significance of Moses and the torah is that they point to Jesus, as Stephen will go on to clarify.

2 True and false worship

Acts 7:42–60

Stephen now turns to the temple, especially the question of true and false worship, engaging with the first accusation against him (6:13). He critiques the generation of Moses who idolatrously worshipped the golden calf using Amos' words (vv. 42–43, quoting Amos 5:25–27) – although he changes 'Damascus' to 'Babylon' to evoke the sixth-century BC Babylonian exile caused by the people's failure to honour God rightly (see 2 Chronicles 36:11–21).

God gave Israel the tabernacle as a place where he met them, and where true worship was offered (vv. 44–45). It was temporary, and Solomon built a temple for God in Jerusalem (v. 47) – and notice again, that the tabernacle was a place where God met people outside the land (v. 44). Stephen quotes Isaiah 66:1–2 (vv. 49–50), to show that God does not live in human-made buildings (v. 48), echoing Solomon's words that the temple could not contain God (1 Kings 8, especially v. 27). Stephen does not criticise the temple in itself but implies that the people are now treating it as an idol by thinking that God's presence was tied there. The temple had its day, but that day is now over – access to God is through Jesus by the Spirit, not through this building.

As the Sanhedrin realise that Stephen is accusing them of failing to worship God aright (v. 54), Jesus himself steps into the story, appearing to Stephen from heaven (v. 55). Stephen identifies Jesus as the 'Son of Man' (v. 56), echoing Daniel's vision (Daniel 7:13–14) of the exalted son of man. Jesus stands as the judge in Stephen's true, heavenly trial, to give his verdict.

Stephen's two prayers (vv. 59–60) highlight who Jesus truly is. First, Jesus is one to whom it is appropriate to offer prayer, whereas first-century Jews would pray to God alone. Second, Jesus has the right to judge and to forgive sins, and so Stephen prays for his murderers' forgiveness, echoing Jesus' action as 'the son of man' in forgiving the paralysed man's sins (Luke 5:20–24); this contrasts sharply with the second-century BC Jewish martyrs, who wanted their pagan enemies punished (see 1 Maccabees 7:14, 16, 19, 31, 35–36). It is through Jesus that people can now come to God, and he welcomes them and transforms their attitudes to be like his – ready to offer forgiveness and to seek others' good.

30 June–6 July

3 Samaritans and the Spirit

Acts 8:1–25

Jesus' mission design involved going beyond Jerusalem to Judaea, Samaria and the end of the earth (1:8). The disciples have not yet left Jerusalem, but the time for that has come. God's means for the expansion is persecution, as the young Saul not only approves of Stephen's murder but seeks to arrest and imprison Jesus-followers (7:58; 8:1, 3). We'll hear much more about Saul soon (9:1–30)!

Saul sets out to destroy the Jesus groups (v. 3). He was convinced they were overturning ancestral Jewish traditions (Galatians 1:13–14), as Stephen's accusers said of him (6:13–14). Many believers flee into Judaea and Samaria (v. 1), the next destinations in Jesus' mission itinerary. Luke focuses on Philip, one of those chosen to resolve disputes among widows (6:5), and his first destination is Samaria.

Judaeans and Samaritans are sworn enemies. Although both trace their ancestry to ancient Israel, and both worship the one true God, practise circumcision and keep scriptural laws, including over food, they differ on key things. Samaritans recognise only the first five scriptural books as authoritative (the Pentateuch), whereas Judaeans accept all the books of our Old Testament. Samaritans have a temple on Mount Gerizim, which Judaeans consider heretical; in turn, Samaritans deem the Jerusalem temple corrupt.

So it's quite something when Philip goes to Samaritans and, through word and deed, sees many baptised as followers of Jesus (vv. 5–8). Philip's 'signs' (v. 6) and his proclamation of Jesus as Messiah (v. 5) show him to be in tune with the apostles. Among the converts is Simon, a magician, and rather than people being amazed at him (v. 11), he is amazed at the gospel and the 'signs and miracles' he sees (v. 13; 'astonished' in NIV is the same Greek word as 'amazed', v. 11).

The surprise in this story is that the Holy Spirit has not yet fallen on these new disciples, breaking the Jerusalem pattern (2:38) – Luke writes verse 16 with raised eyebrows! So Peter and John come and pray for the Spirit to come, and that happens (vv. 15, 17). The Spirit's coming has visible manifestations, for Simon recognises it (v. 18). This 'new Pentecost' is the clearest evidence that the Samaritan believers are genuine, because Jesus has again poured out the Spirit (recall 2:33). It leads to the group evangelising other Samaritan villages (v. 25) – the gospel expansion is starting!

30 June–6 July

4 An Ethiopian eunuch's experience

Acts 8:26–40

Philip is again God's agent in gospel expansion 'to the ends of the earth' (1:8). However, the initiative is God's: God sends Philip into the desert south of Jerusalem with no indication why (v. 26); the Spirit tells him to approach the chariot (v. 29), where he discovers a traveller reading Isaiah (v. 28); the eunuch twice asks for help (vv. 31, 34); in the desert they find a pool suitable for baptism (vv. 36, 38); and the Spirit takes Philip on his way to Caesarea via Azotus (v. 40). This really is a divine appointment!

The eunuch is highly ambiguous. He is an important and powerful man as the chancellor of the Ethiopian queen, the Candace, and thus has a driver for his chariot. That's how he reads while travelling (v. 30) – reading aloud, as usual in the ancient world. As a civil official, the chariot would be an ox-drawn cart rather than the horse-drawn chariots of military officers. He is dark-skinned ('Ethiopian' means 'burnt-face') – modern racism based on skin colour is rare in the ancient world. As a eunuch he is castrated and at least partly dismembered: Luke consistently uses 'the eunuch' to describe him (vv. 27, 34, 36, 38–39). The eunuch would be excluded from full participation in temple worship (Deuteronomy 23:1), and so his visit to Jerusalem 'to worship' would have had limited results – indeed, eunuchs were despised within Judaism. He cannot convert to Judaism as a proselyte, since he cannot be circumcised.

This man at the margins is one whom God seeks. The gospel of Jesus includes those previously excluded as unclean, and Philip interprets scripture to lead the man to faith in Jesus. He's reading Isaiah 53:7–8 as Philip comes alongside, part of a 'servant song' about God's servant who suffers to redeem God's people (vv. 32–33). Philip shows him Jesus starting here – I wonder if they kept reading the Isaiah scroll until Isaiah 56:3–8, promising that eunuchs will be included in God's people.

The gospel needs response, and Philip has evidently explained baptism as expressing that response, for the man asks to be baptised (v. 36). He finds acceptance into the family of Jesus, rather than the barriers in his way at the Jerusalem temple. Later writers see this man as the origin of the church in Ethiopia.

5 Reversal, reversal, reversal

Acts 9:1–30

Saul's encounter with Jesus near Damascus (v. 3) is pivotal in Acts, for through it a ferocious opponent of the believing community (7:58; 8:1, 3) becomes one of its greatest advocates.

First, Jesus transforms Saul's view of Jesus himself from heretic to Lord. Luke does not allow a psychological reading of Saul as one opposing a faith to which he was secretly attracted; from Paul's writings, the opposite is likely (e.g. Philippians 3:4b–6). Through encountering Jesus, Saul changes from a person who knows his own mind (vv. 1–2) to one who must await instructions (v. 6). From controlling others by imprisoning them, Saul enters the control of Jesus and joins Jesus' people. The light of the encounter floods Saul's life with fresh discovery as he discovers that he has been persecuting not merely a group of apostate Jews, but a heavenly figure who is properly called 'Lord' (vv. 4–5).

Second, Jesus transforms Saul from persecutor to proclaimer. Jesus is located in heaven (v. 3; see 1:9–11; 3:21) and rightly addressed as 'Lord' (vv. 5, 10, 13). Both of these features sit comfortably with Acts' emerging picture of Jesus as properly receiving devotion alongside God, echoing Peter's Pentecost declaration (2:36), the dying Stephen's vision of Jesus (7:55), and Stephen's prayer to Jesus (7:59). Saul expresses his transformed understanding of Jesus quickly and publicly (v. 20). He already knew the believers' claims and regarded them as blasphemous prior to the Damascus Road encounter. As an intelligent and educated Jew, he would quickly recognise how his worldview was reorientated around his fresh understanding of Jesus, and thus proclaim him as Messiah and the Son of God (vv. 20, 22).

Third, Jesus transforms Saul from persecutor to persecuted. Ananias is told that Saul will suffer for Jesus' name (v. 16), and this is played out in Damascus, as Jews who were expecting to welcome his campaign against the believers turn against Saul and seek his life (vv. 21, 23). It is also seen in Jerusalem as Hellenistic Jews seek to kill him (v. 29). In both places, his new sisters and brothers ensure his safe escape (vv. 25, 30) – Saul's family allegiance has changed through his baptism (v. 18). The suffering which Saul experiences in these two cities is the precursor of many later events, where his ministry is received with controversy, debate and often physical attack.

6 On the road with Peter

Acts 9:31–43

Luke highlights that both women and men become believers (5:14; 8:3, 12; 9:2), just as in his gospel he often pairs a story about a man with one about a woman (e.g. Zechariah and Mary, Luke 1:5–80; the shepherd and the woman, Luke 15:3–10). Here, through Peter, Jesus heals a man, Aeneas (vv. 32–35), and raises a woman from death, Tabitha/Dorcas (vv. 36–42). These stories also continue the theme of gospel expansion, for Peter is visiting churches at the coastal limit of Judaea (v. 31 and see 1:8).

The Lord has got to Lydda and Joppa before Peter, for there are believers there already (v. 32). Some may well be Pentecost pilgrims who became disciples then (Lydda and Joppa are in Judaea, 2:9), or have fled Jerusalem because of persecution and evangelised these towns (8:1, 4). Peter's words also make clear that it is the exalted Jesus who is at work (v. 34), echoing the healing of the man at the temple (3:6, 12, 16; 4:10). Similarly, Peter prays for Tabitha, kneeling to indicate intensity of prayer, before calling her to get up (v. 40). The contrast with Jesus' healing of Jairus' daughter is striking, for Jesus does not pray, but simply commands her to get up (Luke 8:54). Peter does not act in his own power like Jesus but is dependent on Jesus acting from heaven.

Tabitha's raising and Aeneas' healing are examples of the 'times of refreshing' which Peter announced in the temple (3:19). They show that the exalted Jesus is at work transforming this damaged creation and prefiguring Jesus' return, when he will 'restore everything' (3:21). It is Jesus' exaltation as Messiah (= 'Christ', v. 34), raised from the dead, and Lord (vv. 35, 42) that makes these remarkable events both possible and significant.

Such remarkable events require and facilitate response, too – in both towns, people become believers by 'turning' to the Lord or 'believing' in the Lord (vv. 35, 42). Both verbs echo Peter's Pentecostal summary of conversion: repentance (turning) and faith expressed in baptism (2:38). Luke does not tell these stories merely for their own sake, but to show how God's mission expands, driven by Jesus' heavenly action and carried out through Jesus' chosen agents. Not only is the mission expanding, but geography is being transformed as the heavenly dimension of reality overlaps with the earthly.

Guidelines

Saul Steinberg drew the world looking from New York's 9th Avenue. 10th Avenue is quite large, the Hudson River smaller – and (ever smaller) New Jersey, Kansas City, Las Vegas and Los Angeles (on the west coast), the Pacific Ocean, following by tiny China, Japan and Russia (see it here: tinyurl.com/3cuh5tvf). We may laugh at this parochial view, but such myopia afflicts many of us Christians today. We engage with the concerns we and our family, and our church have, and don't look more widely. Acts 1—9 invites us to do that.

The church's expansion from Jerusalem into Judaea and Samaria is the story of God acting. It took persecution for many believers to leave the city (8:1), resulting in growth and evangelism (8:4). Philip went to the hated Samaritans and saw God act remarkably alongside his proclamation of Jesus as Messiah (8:5–8), leading to the Spirit coming on the converts through Peter and John (8:14–17). It took an angel and the Spirit to guide Philip to a desert meeting with the Ethiopian (8:26, 29), and then on to Azotus and Caesarea (8:40). It took Jesus acting from heaven to call Saul to follow him, and to become a key figure in reaching beyond Judaism to Gentiles (9:1–9, 15–16).

Acts is full of human characters, but they are not the drivers of the believing community's growth and expansion – God is. Jesus acts from heaven, including through the Holy Spirit, to draw people into his church. It's all too easy, as we think about enabling our church to grow and develop, to focus on what we do, but that would be a mistake. The heavenly dimension – an expanded geography – is as vital today as then. How are you and your church recognising this and inviting Jesus to act from heaven and by his Spirit today?

FURTHER READING

Beverly Gaventa, *Acts* (Abingdon, 2003).
Tom Wright, *The Challenge of Acts* (SPCK/Zondervan, 2024).

Lamentations

Victoria Omotoso

Have you ever shed tears until it felt like there was nothing left within you? The author of Lamentations captures this profound sense of grief as he bears witness to the devastation of his beloved city. Lamentations, traditionally attributed to the prophet Jeremiah, often referred to as 'the weeping prophet', offers a poignant response to the destruction of Jerusalem through five poems. The first four chapters follow an acrostic pattern, mirroring the Hebrew alphabet of 22 letters. Chapters 1, 2, and 4 contain one verse for each letter, while Chapter 3 comprises 22 stanzas, each corresponding to a letter. Chapter 5, although consisting of 22 verses, deviates from the acrostic structure.

The response to the destruction in Lamentations follows a structured pattern, allowing the author to express his emotions and reactions to the unfolding tragedy. Firstly, Lamentations serves as a form of protest, providing a platform to speak out against the suffering endured. Secondly, it serves as a tool for processing emotions, encompassing feelings of grief, anger and even glimpses of hope. Within the pages of Lamentations, the author finds a space to articulate his confusion regarding the events unfolding before him. Ultimately, Lamentations grants dignity to human suffering, offering a sanctuary for the full expression of sorrow and lamentation.

At the time this letter was written, Jerusalem had endured the most catastrophic event in its recorded history. Once a city of triumph, ruled by prophets and kings, it now lies in ruins; the people who would once fill the streets with laughter and singing are now sitting in the dirt, looking for scraps to eat; death and the sounds of wailing are flooding these streets. The author unveils the catastrophe that has brought Jerusalem to her knees and acknowledges that the consequences of their sin has brought about this downfall. Thus, the author realises that his part of the covenant has failed and wrestles with the hope of trusting God in the middle of the storm. Lamentations serves as a constant reminder that we can protest, pray and contest with the circumstances we face knowing that God is listening, knowing that God sees.

Unless otherwise stated, Bible quotations are taken from the NLT.

1 Jerusalem, the widow

Lamentations 1:1–10; Jeremiah 2:13

In the opening lines, Jerusalem emerges as a poignant figure of misery and grief. Personified as a widow, the term extends beyond a simple depiction of her relationship with YHWH as her husband. Instead, it conveys the profound sense of desolation, isolation and misery that envelops the city. This metaphor of widowhood encapsulates Jerusalem's state of separation, both from its past glory and from any semblance of present significance. The stark contrast between its former grandeur and its current desolation amplifies the palpable sense of loss that pervades the narrative.

The author further elaborates on the profound loneliness that grips the city, highlighting the betrayal by other 'lovers' and 'friends', and the dissolution of the security and comfort once found in Jerusalem. This passage offers a poignant insight into the heart of the devastation, revealing a recurring cycle wherein Jerusalem seeks solace and security in alternative sources, turns to other gods and succumbs to the sin of self-sufficiency – ultimately leading to its downfall. This echoes God's earlier warnings to Judah through the prophets, reminding them of their forgetfulness toward the God who delivered them from Egypt.

'For my people have done two evil things: They have abandoned me – the fountain of living water. And they have dug for themselves cracked cisterns that can hold no water at all!' (Jeremiah 2:13). The people had forsaken the source of all things – the living water – for a cracked cistern. This imagery paints a vivid picture of their departure from God's abundant provision to relying on a flawed and inadequate substitute. Just as a cistern with holes cannot retain rainwater for future use, turning to idols led them to store up broken promises.

Lamentations finds us in a similar predicament – a people who have drifted away from the life-giving source. It prompts reflection on how often we, too, are tempted to stray from the Source of Living Water. We invest our efforts in transient systems such as wealth, religious practices or ego, only to find them insufficient, temporary and unreliable. Unlike these temporary cisterns, the living water offered by God is enduring and fulfilling, quenching our deepest thirsts.

2 The people vs YHWH

Lamentations 2:3–7, 17–22

Lamentations presents a stark cause-and-effect scenario: Israel's failure to uphold their loyalty to YHWH results in devastating consequences. In verse 5, the heart of the matter is laid bare: 'Yes, the Lord has vanquished Israel like an enemy.' This marks a full-scale conflict, with the city rendered utterly defenceless. The Lord, turning his back on his people, engages in a battle against them – a fearsome prospect, as Hebrews 10:31 warns, 'It is a terrible thing to fall into the hands of the living God.' The Lord dismantles the city's strongest defences and symbols of pride, including its fortresses and even the temple – the very dwelling place of God.

The destruction of the temple, Solomon's magnificent structure that once stood as the pride and joy of the people, marked a profound shift. It symbolised God's apparent rejection of his people, signalling his withdrawal from their midst. The tangible loss of the temple emphasised the absence of God's presence among them – an absence keenly felt by the entire nation. The repercussions of such a loss, whether on a national, communal or individual level, are dire. Consider Samson, who, when diverted from his divine purpose, remained oblivious to the departure of the Lord's presence from him (Judges 16:20), or King Saul, whose disobedience led to the Lord's withdrawal and subsequent downfall (1 Samuel 16:14–23). In Lamentations, the temple – the heart of culture, worship and communion with God – was gone. It is a stark lesson for us today that our places are not as important as our priorities of worship. The posture of our hearts is what God sees, not where we are. The prophet Isaiah warns the people with this message from the Lord, 'And so the Lord says, "These people say they are mine. They honour me with their lips, but their hearts are far from me. And their worship of me is nothing but man-made rules learned by rote."' (Isaiah 29:13).

The sincerity of our heart is what matters most to God. The people of Israel had forgotten their first love: they had run away from their Source and were finding their security elsewhere. Now God had become their enemy and they realised that they only had God as their help. It is a horrible, terrifying scene towards the end of chapter 2, a stark reminder of the path of destruction that sin can bring.

3 The darkness

Lamentations 3:1–20

Survivors exist in a delicate balance, a tension that straddles the line between the trauma of the past and the glimmer of hope on the horizon. Positioned in the heart of Lamentations, chapter 3 serves as a poignant reflection on both the collective devastation and the individual's personal anguish. Here, the author, himself a survivor, vividly portrays the feeling of being abandoned by God and plunged into darkness. The Hebrew term used, *choshek*, conveys not just physical darkness, but also a sense of obscurity and uncertainty – a place where clarity and visibility are sorely lacking.

The author grapples with the realisation that his sense of abandonment stems from God's own anger. In scripture, knowledge of God is equated to light, a profound intimacy rather than merely intellectual comprehension. This intimate knowing reflects a relationship akin to marriage, where covenant and intimacy are deeply intertwined. The depiction of Jerusalem as a widow in the first chapter underscores the profound loss experienced when such a bond is severed. Chapter 3 delves into the author's struggle with this sense of separation from God, feeling engulfed by darkness.

However, while darkness typically symbolises despair, it also serves as a transformative space in our spiritual journey. During such times, we undergo a process akin to growing pains – necessary for our spiritual development. These periods of darkness afford us the opportunity to shed distractions and reset our perspective on life. In the physical realm, darkness plays a vital role in sustaining life. Observe the womb, a place of darkness that is essential for fostering life and preparing us for the light of day. Similarly, in our spiritual journey, darkness can serve as a catalyst for deeper understanding of God. Despite moments when God's presence may seem obscured, the truth remains: he is omnipresent, as affirmed by the psalmist: 'If I go up to heaven, you are there; if I go down to the grave, you are there' (Psalm 139:8).

4 Hope

Lamentations 3:21–27

I have long held to what I refer to as the 'But God' phenomenon – a belief that despite any struggle, suffering, or pain, there's always a 'But God' moment. That is to say that God still makes his faithfulness known even in the darkest moment. Corrie ten Boom, a survivor of the Holocaust, said, 'I've experienced His presence in the deepest darkest hell that men can create… I have tested the promises of the Bible, and believe me, you can count on them.' God's faithfulness is a constant in the messiness and the darkness of life. As a survivor of one of the most horrific occurrences in living memory, Corrie ten Boom was able to rest in the promises of God and find hope in the darkness. The author of Lamentations has expressed the devastation and despair of the remains for the city. He has felt the anguish of the darkness, the separation of God – 'yet'. This word changes everything. 'Yet' as a conjunction implies that there is a contrast, something unexpected has happened. The Hebrew word for 'yet' denotes a returning, to turn back. It shows that although this terrible event has happened there is a process of returning. Verse 21 says, 'Yet I still dare to hope when I remember this.' The author has a ray of hope in the middle of the darkness.

I often wear a 'hope' pin enamel on my lapels. It's always a great conversation starter and, as I've conversed with others about my 'hope' pins, I've come to realise that we are all in need of hope. I've always imagined hope or try to characterise it as a lighthouse. In the darkness and crashing waves, a lighthouse stands as a beacon of light shining through. I see hope as that, a light in the darkness, and I believe the author of Lamentations sees the same. Here in the middle of the devastation and destruction, the grief he has witnessed, he is reminded of God's faithfulness.

As Christians, we often suffer from spiritual amnesia: we tend to forget what God has already done for us, the journey he has brought us through already. We forget and begin to dwell on the current circumstances of struggle. Now, it is fine to acknowledge our problems. If it weren't, we wouldn't have the book of Lamentations, which expresses the human nature of suffering. But what this chapter teaches us is that even in the middle of the darkness, 'the faithful love of the Lord never ends! His mercies never cease. Great is his faithfulness; his mercies begin afresh each morning' (vv. 22–23). We need to continuously remember God's faithfulness in the past that will bring hope for the uncertainty of tomorrow. God is always faithful.

5 *Hésed*

Lamentations 3: 31–33, 40–42, 52–58

This term *hésed* poses a challenge to translate in English. It is popularly translated as 'unfailing love'; we can also use words such as 'kindness', 'love' and 'goodness'. *Hésed* moves beyond the capacity of appropriating kindness and love; it also involves loyalty. A covenant underpins this loyalty; although Israel kept turning away, God's *hésed* remains steadfastly loyal to them. This unfailing love epitomises *hésed*; it is steadfast and never disappoints. While all other loves may falter, betray, or disappoint us, *hésed* remains unwavering.

This 'unfailing love' is what the author of Lamentations puts his hope in: 'For no one is abandoned by the Lord forever. Though he brings grief, he also shows compassion because of the greatness of his unfailing love' (vv. 31–32). The *hésed* of the Lord is what sustains hope even in the middle of God's judgement. The author knows that God's *hésed* will not forget them. Here, the author speaks on behalf of the community of the awareness of their sin and the call to return to the Lord (vv. 40–42).

This collective call of retuning requires a deep introspection of their hearts – it is an issue of heart posture. With the temple destroyed, as we've seen, God does not prioritise our places of worship, or the rituals of worship, if our heart posture is not in a place of surrender to his will. The people have come to this realisation and begin the process of returning – returning to the One who turned away from them and from whom they turned away. Yet, within his unfailing love, there exists room for repentance, reconciliation and restoration. This is a beautiful picture of the ultimate salvation price, that as we have turned away (Isaiah 53:6), the Lord in his *hésed* had made a way for us to return. Jesus embodied the ultimate manifestation of *hésed* – love unfailing – being *hésed* made flesh. His sacrificial act brought about the hope we hold today. This is why the author of Lamentations finds hope; in *hésed*, there is assurance to bask in the love of the Father.

The author merges their own personal experiences to image the situation of the nation. Even in the depths of despair and devastation, God can rescue. Jeremiah, attributed as the author of Lamentations, was thrown into a cistern (Jeremiah 38) and called out to the Lord to rescue him. Here the author parallels this personal trauma with the nation's situation: a delving into deep sin, cast into a place of despair, yet God, in the capacity of *hésed*, comes to save.

6 The uncertain

Lamentations 5

The final poem of Lamentations forms a solemn liturgy for the national calamity that has occurred. Unlike the previous chapters, this conclusion does not use the acrostic pattern, although it still consists of 22 verses. It is almost as if the orderly expressions of grief and pain have been set aside and there is a desperate last call to address God. The people call for a remembrance (v. 1). They have known that God brings people into remembrance, from Noah to their father, Abraham, who was remembered by God to have a child, to the people freed from slavery in Egypt – God remembers. For God to remember does not mean he has forgotten; rather, it signifies God's deliberate timing in intervening. Even when his presence seems elusive, God remains vigilant, awaiting the opportune moment to act.

Remembrance is always working hand in hand with action; it involves the process through which God decides that he will intervene. For as the prophet Isaiah states, 'Listen! The Lord's arm is not too weak to save you, nor is his ear too deaf to hear you call' (Isaiah 59:1). While we may feel like God's rescue is beyond our reach, it is often due to our own shortcomings: the ways in which we have depended on other sources of strength, or the way we have stored our water in 'broken cisterns', whether that be looking to our job or our relationships for security. If there was one lesson to learn, the COVID-19 pandemic has underscored the transient nature of worldly security; in the blink of an eye, everything can change. The pandemic revealed the fragility of our world and our collective vulnerability as individuals. It prompted us to recognise that our true security lies in the One who is unchanging, the One who will 'remain the same forever!' (v. 19).

Lamentations acknowledges the sovereignty of God and brings a prayer of restoration and remembrance. While this prayer quantifies the grief that has afflicted the city, faith is still maintained that God can remember and restore them. However, a pivotal moment arises when the author questions whether God's anger persists. The final poem concludes with an enigmatic examination, perhaps hinting at God's perceived indifference. Throughout the book, God remains silent, yet the author persists in voicing his prayers. This persistent prayer sustains hope, culminating in eventual restoration. While God does not respond, the author nonetheless keeps persevering in the hope that his voice will be heard. Persistent prayer will fan the flame of hope. Of course, we know the end of the story: restoration does finally come.

Guidelines

Lamentations is a guide for believers to openly express their griefs and concerns to God. It recognises the effects of what it means to be in broken human condition. Sin is a by-product of the broken state of creation we currently occupy, and the impact is utterly devastating. Lamentations names the devastation, calls it by name, and still provides a ray of hope in the middle of the darkness.

As we engage with Lamentations, it prompts us to know that the *hésed* of the Lord remains a constant in the middle of the mess we often find ourselves in.

- How does Lamentations resonate with your understanding of God's relationship with his people?
- Have you ever felt hesitant to voice your complaints to God?
- Reflecting on Lamentations, can you identify moments where you have fallen short and acknowledge the need for repentance and restoration?

Great is his faithfulness!

FURTHER READING

Rachael Newham, *And Yet: Finding joy in lament* (SPCK, 2021).

Selina Stone, *Tarry a While: Wisdom from Black spirituality for people of faith* (SPCK, 2024).

Christopher J.H. Wright, *The Message of Lamentations: Honest to God* (IVP Academic, 2015).

War and peace

Valerie Hobbs

I was born and raised among Christo-fascists in the United States, a growing community that seeks to bring about the return of Jesus Christ through their reclamation of every 'high place', every sphere of earthly power and influence both nationally and globally. I have written about the everyday violence of this ideology, this life without love, among such people of war, in my latest book, *No Love in War* (Mayfly Books, 2023). It's important to speak clearly and confidently about such urgent things, as the pendulum of the world's politics continues to swing towards the extremist right. As parts of our western world continue to manufacture and sell weapons, as the world wages its wars, as this brutality continues to infiltrate the Christian church, our pulpits and pews, this and next week's Bible notes focus, first, on the idolatry and absurdity of all such bloodshed. And then on the only answer to all our human hate: the love and perfect peace that Jesus Christ brings to the wandering world, by the authority of his Father in heaven, through the unquenchable power of the Spirit.

A final point: You'll notice that I have avoided the name 'Israel' in my notes this week, choosing instead the name 'Yisrael,' a transliteration of the Hebrew name God gave to Jacob in Genesis 32. While not entirely unproblematic, I take this step in order to distinguish clearly between the people of God in the Hebrew Bible and the modern state of Israel. In keeping with this, these notes are dedicated especially to our Palestinian brothers and sisters in Christ who have for many decades suffered the brutal effects of Zionism in Gaza and the occupied West Bank.

Unless otherwise stated, Bible quotations are taken from the NASB (1995).

1 Peaceable, faithful, even a mother

1 Samuel 1:9–18; 2 Samuel 20:1–19

In the books of Samuel, we encounter a lot of men and a lot of violence. Men arguing and betraying. Men fighting over and oppressing women. Men running around and stabbing each other with swords. Men plotting and scheming. Men acting like cowards. Men acting absurdly. But lest we forget, that is the point! These men simply aren't enough to do what needs doing.

But here is another point. 1 Samuel begins not with those men but with a mother in Yisrael, Hannah. Hannah longs to have children and goes to the temple in Shiloh to plead with the Lord. So close to God is Hannah that she speaks in a language without words, in a voice inaudible to men. Such is her state that the Levite Priest Eli thinks she is drunk. But of course, Hannah is *not* drunk. And in her holy state of communion with God, she rebukes the Priest.

In 2 Samuel 20, we encounter another wise woman. The background to this is a worthless fellow, Sheba, who sets his sights on David's increasingly weak leadership and seizes his moment. He starts by parading around, spreading disloyalty to the king, blasting on his trumpet all kinds of false teaching, all around town.

Poor David realises Sheba is real trouble, worse even than his wayward son Absalom, and he sends Joab the Scheming General after him. Sheba ends up hiding in the city of Abel Beth-Maacah, and Joab starts an all-out assault on the whole city. All this violence for one man? Oh yes indeed.

The city of Abel (!) might have been flattened in this machismo mayhem were it not for a certain wise woman. She calls out from the city to General Joab and, Hannah-like, rebukes him. And like Eli, Joab can do nothing in the face of such strength except say, 'I am listening.' (20:17).

In the light of God's redemptive story, I can't help but think it was wise, peace-seeking, mighty women of the Hebrew Bible like these who inspired Paul's counsel about the conduct of *both* men *and* women (1 Timothy 3; Titus 2). This isn't some 'Dare to be a Daniel' message, nor is it oppressively gendered. Is not Paul here calling the church to put away all absurd violence, rather to behave like people of God's promise, fulfilled in the perfect work of Christ, a people who are 'peaceable, faithful, even a mother' (20:19)?

2 High places

Matthew 4:1–11; 17:1–13

Repetition is God's signposting. In the books of Kings alone, for example, God refers to 'high places' 15 times. In many places in the Bible, 'high places' refer to places of worship, often on hills and mountains, often idolatrous, though not always so. We frequently find them in summaries of a king's character, demonstrating that God holds the king responsible for the spiritual state of his people. 1 Kings 3:1–4, for example, draws our attention to Solomon's inadequacy. We find the same in 1 Kings 22:41–43, this time about Jehoshaphat.

But there is still more to these high places. At Babel, we learn about humanity's instinct to reach heaven by human hands. Elsewhere, we meet this message in subtler ways. We encounter it in the physical height of the Nephilim and their descendants. This prepares us for Saul's double whammy in the high places department, the first in reference to his physical stature. God even has to warn Samuel (and us!) not to be taken in by his handsome looks (1 Samuel 16:7). And then notice where Samuel meets Saul: on the roof of Saul's house, a symbolic site of sin that appears again later, in David's adulterous desires.

A picture is emerging, is it not? In Genesis, Satan had promised Adam and Eve a perverted dominion and in so doing, cast us all to the earth. From then till now, Satan has continued to tempt us with his endlessly empty offers. All who choose his way will be 'as grass on the housetops is scorched before it is grown up' (2 Kings 19:26).

What to do? How can we return to the blessings of heaven?

We catch a glimpse of the answer at times, as when Moses climbs the mountain. Here is God's sign of the One who would defeat Satan on the high places of the wilderness (Matthew 4). Here is the One who would climb a high mountain with his disciples, witness Moses and Elijah in glory, and hear the voice of God his Father (Matthew 17).

In all this, God offers us union with this One, the Lord and Saviour Jesus Christ, whose humiliating death on a hill sets us on the high places, no longer condemned to the dust of this earth but raised not to domination but to newness of life, in all its flourishing.

14–20 July

3 Troublers of Yisrael

1 Kings 22:1–28

I love the plain-spoken prophets, bold and blunt, unsettlers of powerful people. When King Ahab of Yisrael finally sees Elijah, that elusive truth-teller, he says, wearily, 'Is that you, you troubler of Yisrael?' (1 Kings 18:17). Micaiah is another favourite among the troublemaker prophets. His brief story takes place not long after Elijah comes on the scene, during the reign of King Jehoshaphat of Judah. Three years (see John 2:19–21) have passed mercifully without war. Yet the childish and covetous King Ahab of Yisrael, having stolen Naboth's vineyard, craves more land, this time the city of Ramoth-gilead, dominating Judah by involving them in his quest for war.

But Jehoshaphat hesitates, even after Ahab's prophets assure them of victory. So in comes Micaiah, who lives up to his rebel rep and ultimately reveals the truth, relaying a vision of the heavenly court and God's power over the fate of land-grabbing Ahab and his sinful supremacy over Judah. Indeed, Micaiah's prophecy defies the yes-man prophets and spells out disaster for Ahab.

According to scholar Catherine Quine, especially noteworthy is this prophecy's challenge to Near Eastern understanding of warfare, where an earthly king's victory or defeat corresponded to victory or defeat for the divine, in Yisrael's case Yahweh. Micaiah's vision of the courts of heaven presents a God whose supreme authority supersedes the interests of earthly kings.

Unsurprisingly, like so many modern political rulers who claim divine sanction for their warmongering, King Ahab can't handle the truth. The room is in uproar. The prophet Zedekiah accuses Micaiah of blasphemy, striking him across the cheek, and Ahab throws Micaiah in prison.

We find more so-called troublemakers in the New Testament, more threats to the self-interests of powerful and greedy people. Chief among them is Jesus Christ, likewise struck in the face by religious leaders, likewise accused of blasphemy. 'Prophesy to us, Messiah. Who hit you?', they mocked (Matthew 26:68, NIV).

The Bible doesn't tell us what happened to the prophet Micaiah after his imprisonment, though we do hear of King Ahab's cowardly death, confirming Micaiah's word of prophecy. So too would Jesus' words about himself be confirmed upon his own death. Micaiah's final words echo in our ears, calling us to believe: 'Listen, all you people.'

4 Iron and rock

1 Corinthians 10:1–3

Along with other favourite themes in the Bible – like grapes and hair – I've been tracking rocks and iron. So imagine my joy at this intrigue in yesterday's text:

> *Then Zedekiah the son of Chenaanah made horns of iron for himself and said, 'This is what the Lord says: 'With these you will gore the Arameans until they are destroyed!''*
>
> 1 KINGS 22:11 (NASB 2020)

The Bible's symbolic use of iron begins with Tubal-Cain in Genesis 4:22. Here God reveals that this descendent of Abel's murderer was a forger of all implements of bronze and iron. 1 Kings 8:51 explains more, that Tubal-Cain's metalwork belongs to the slavers of Egypt, 'that iron-smelting furnace' (NIV). It is the joy of giants, descendants of the serpent, like King Og of Bashan who slept on a bedstead of iron (Deuteronomy 3:11). It is the work and weapon of the enemies of God (Judges 1:19), used by King David as punishment against the Ammonites, in the form of enslavement in iron mines (2 Samuel 12:29–31).

As such, ironwork by God's people is notably limited, if not outright forbidden. At various points, God tells his people not to shape rocks with iron (Deuteronomy 27:5; Joshua 8:31). In the construction of the Temple, 'there was no sound of hammer, axe, or any other iron tool at the building site.' (1 Kings 6:7, NLT).

Why is this? As Paul tells us, the rock Joshua used to build an altar, the stone builders used for Solomon's Temple, the rock Moses struck and struck again in anger, the stone rejected by Babel's builders, that Rock was Christ.

And the iron? These are warfare's accoutrements, the nails that pierced our Saviour's hands, the spear soldiers plunged into his side (John 20:25), the chains that imprisoned God's people, the saws that hacked them in two, the swords that saw their earthly end (Hebrews 11).

While the prophet Zedekiah forges horns of iron for war, from the prophet Micaiah's mouth comes a rather different weapon, a spiritual one, forged in the armies of heaven, cutting straight to the heart of all oppressors. Each rock is a citizen of heaven, guarded with love, 'built on the foundation of the apostles and prophets, with Christ Jesus himself as the chief cornerstone' (Ephesians 2:19–20, NIV; see also Ezekiel 11:19).

5 Heights of earth, heights of heaven

Mark 2:1–12

Today's reading returns to high places. We humans, forever tempted by power and the wars necessary to hoard it, will always need the reminder. Jesus is living in Capernaum, a hub for his earthly ministry. Capernaum means 'disorderly accumulation of objects'. And indeed, Jesus is all about restoring order.

It's a familiar story. Four persistent men want Jesus to heal their paralytic friend, but they can't get into the room, 'not even near the door' (v. 2). So they climb to the roof, dig an opening and lower their friend's pallet. Their thoughts are initially on earthly healing. They have a noble goal, an angelic one even: the blessing of a healthy body for a friend unable to help himself. So they ascend to the roof to claim it.

Yet Jesus does not meet them on the high places. Instead, they must lower their friend down to the dust, down to the feet of the Saviour. And just look at how Jesus' priorities reveal his kingdom plan. His first response offers the man at his feet *not* the high places of earth but something altogether more eternal: forgiveness (Matthew 6:33).

But for those watching in unbelief, even the grumbling scribes 'sitting there and reasoning in their hearts' (v. 6), Jesus next offers a corporeal sign, an earthly ascension from the paralytic man's pallet, a physical manifestation of a future triumph.

In Jesus Christ, the Bible's stories of high places find their forever home. Through his own glorious humiliation, Jesus models for us the way to our future in the heights of heaven. He asks us to repent at his feet in the dust of a fallen creation, to destroy not the high places of this passing earth but rather the ones within our own hearts, to love the Lord our God with all our heart, soul, strength and mind, and our neighbour as ourselves. And in all, because of his work alone, to ascend with him the mountain of the Lord.

And what awaits us after that? Not only spiritual reign with Christ in the heavenly places, ours now at this very moment if we believe (Ephesians 1:3), but the heights of a new heaven and earth when he comes again. In that order exactly.

6 The bramble king

Judges 9:8–20

If you are a lover of animals and the natural world, the Bible has a lot to offer you. The list in Isaiah 34 is quite something, for starters. Pelicans! Hedgehogs! Owls! Ravens! Jackals! Ostriches! Hairy goats! Wolves! Thorns, weeds and thistles! And does your heart not skip a beat when you encounter the night monster?

Be careful though. This is no jolly nature walk.

At the world's beginning, God set up a paradise where humans exercised peaceful oversight in the natural world. But Adam and Eve upended that order, all hell broke loose, and the world is not as it should be, full of the hate and violence of war. The wild things in the biblical narrative often represent the failure of God's people to look after God's creation in love.

Take brambles, for instance, in Jotham's parable today. What is their meaning?

The Garden of Eden, that sad place where God curses the ground with thorns and thistles, helps us understand (Genesis 3:18). Isaiah (34:13) and Hosea (10:8) speak of this too, of places where wildness rules, where prickly, pervasive and persistent vines of all sorts crawl in, take over, choke the life out of places of love, beauty, strength and worship.

We jump ahead to Jesus' parable of the sower (Matthew 13:7–22), where the 'worry of the world and the deceitfulness of wealth' (v. 22) choke and stifle one who has heard the truth.

At the time of the judges, Yisrael was impatient. They wanted an earthly king, and they chose Abimelech, the bramble king. Yet at the place where Jotham warned Yisrael that their violent bramble king would be a thorn in their flesh, would even consume them with fire, there Jesus later told the Samaritan woman about another bramble king. A ram caught in a thicket. The Creator of the Universe who would die in the shade of a bramble crown. Not a bramble king but a conqueror of brambles (Isaiah 10:17–20).

14–20 July

Guidelines

This week's notes have considered some of the way's the biblical text confronts us with the absurdities of war and its roots in greed and arrogance. I hope you've seen some of the many ways God turns all earthly strength on its head, subverting it, even at times mocking it, all in divine pursuit of a radical equality that defies all our human hierarchies.

As you finish this week, I challenge you to consider the ways that an oppressive ideology demanding infiltration of and domination over all structures of society may have crept in to your own thinking or the thinking of Christians in your community. Clues to this thinking include references to such things as:

- recovering a nation's 'lost Christian heritage';
- God's special plan for a specific geographic region ('God has big plans for Sheffield');
- Christians having a duty to amass influence in whatever profession they are working in.

As and when you encounter any such messages, I hope these notes will encourage you, first, to rest in the perfect work of Jesus Christ. And then! Embrace the freedom Christ gives you now to act with boldness to serve and empower the poor, the sick, the disenfranchised, the oppressed. We do this not to bring about heaven on earth nor to summon Christ's return but rather to offer our neighbour a taste of the richness, the fullness of our salvation. Tomorrow's bread given to us today.

1 The raven and the dove

1 Kings 17:1–7; Matthew 3:13–17

The story of Elijah and the ravens pulls on multiple narrative threads. Along with the owl, the pelican and the ostrich, the raven marks the desolation of Edom. It craves the wandering eye. Ravens are a sign of wildness and lost dominion. As such, ravens were forbidden as food for the Yisraelites.

The story's location is also familiar. The brook of Cherith is east of the Jordan, 'well watered everywhere like the garden of the Lord' (Genesis 13:10, NRSV). Lot cannot resist it and settles there, as do some of the tribes of Yisrael.

This easterly land may seem enticing, then. But it is unsettling, incomplete. After Lot, Moses leads the Yisraelites there but is not allowed to cross the Jordan as punishment for striking the rock. In this same place, then, even though the ravens provide Elijah with bread and meat, this true prophet cannot stay. The waters soon dry up, and the Lord tells him to move on.

God has told parts of this story before. At the end of Genesis 7, Noah and his family are in the ark, they alone with the animals saved through God's watery judgement of the whole world. And at this point, something curious happens, a kind of mirroring of heaven and earth.

The text says that God remembered Noah, his family and all the animals. And just as the Spirit of God hovered over the surface of the waters at the world's creation, God causes a wind to pass over the flooded earth, and the waters subside. The ark comes to rest upon the mountains of Ararat.

Noah responds to this supernatural act by sending out the raven. And like the wind, like the ravens that fed Elijah, Noah's raven 'flew here and there until the water was dried up from the earth' (Genesis 8:6–7).

As the raven wanders, before the flood waters recede, Noah releases another bird, a dove. Though she too finds no resting place, the dove returns. And Noah sends her out again and again until she brings the olive leaf of peace and flies away to rest, awaiting her descent to Jesus Christ at his baptism.

In the raven and the dove, we encounter restlessness and rest, earth and heaven, here and there. And though we are fixed anxiously between the two, in Jesus Christ the dove and raven meet in perfect peace (Song of Songs 5:11–12). Here is rest for our restless hearts.

2 More valuable than many sparrows

Matthew 10:16–31

In the British Museum, you can visit the Taylor Prism, which lists the campaigns of King Sennacherib of the Neo-Assyrian empire, until the start of his final war against Babylon. Notably, the prism includes a description of Sennacherib's dealings with Hezekiah, King of Judah in 701 BC: 'As for Hezekiah, I shut him up like a caged bird in his royal city of Jerusalem.'

The figurative language here is provocative in light of the Bible's use of birds. Their symbolic meaning has less to do with scientific accuracy and more about their meaningfulness within Hebrew cultural mythology. For example, in Isaiah, the pelicans, owls, ravens and ostriches, along with other plants and animals seen as wild, represent wandering, the failure to exercise dominion.

But with other birds are other meanings. Small birds like pigeons, sparrows and turtledoves were offerings the poor brought to the Temple, likewise the meat of the poor (Luke 2:24). For this reason, small birds often symbolised provision and reliance on God.

But this humble provision was not entirely material. As birds are often metaphors for the soul, the Bible often uses them to evoke the promise of heaven. There, like the birds of the air, God's people would at last have a place to lay their heads (Luke 9:58). The spiritual home which Christ secured through his victory over death would take on substance. The people of God, poor in spirit, would be set free from the cage of this life.

All this we carry with us when we meet Jesus' words in Matthew 10.

The sparrow, the pigeon, the turtledove – all small birds are pictures God's Word provides of the care our loving heavenly Father has for us. Though we are vulnerable to violence for a time, as birds are, not one of us falls without God's notice. And though like Hezekiah we are caged for a time in the kingdom of this world, likewise, as in Hezekiah's time, our deliverance will come about suddenly.

3 Hezekiah and the thing that came about suddenly

2 Chronicles 29:31–35, 31:6–10; Mark 6:30–44

Here I am, reading along in Chronicles, when, just like that, 'the people rejoiced over what God had prepared for the people, because the thing came about suddenly.' (2 Chronicles 29:36).

The reign of Hezekiah has many glorious gems, like a double Passover feast (2 Chronicles 30:26–27). Hezekiah also leads God's people in kingdom work. They tear down the idols, high places and altars. They reinstate the priesthood, to minister, give thanks and praise. And then: the 'tithe of sacred gifts' (2 Chronicles 31:6). Out of what God gives, the people give. They give, they give so freely, that the priests have enough to eat with plenty left over.

And here we leave 2 Chronicles, beyond the exile of Judah and their return, beyond 400 years of waiting for God.

On we go, until we reach the place where Jesus begins his ministry. Where he sends his twelve disciples to gather the people for a new Exodus. Where he tells them to travel light as the Yisraelites did. Where, like Moses, Jesus crosses the Sea of Galilee with his disciples to a desolate place.

Here, in Jewish territory, a crowd begins to gather, and Jesus teaches them until it's quite late, until they are all quite hungry. Knowing their need, he commands the crowd to sit, and they recline as if at a king's banquet 'on the green grass' (Mark 6:39), a sign of wilderness transformed. Likewise, in Gentile territory, Jesus meets another famished crowd, directs them to sit on the ground and rest (Mark 8:6).

Here and there, with Jews and Gentiles alike, Jesus takes the meagre gifts of food, blesses it and gives it to his disciples. In both places, all eat. All are satisfied. So it was, just as in Hezekiah's day, that out of what God had given the people, out of what they returned to him, there was enough for everyone and plenty left over, a sign of safe passage through the wilderness, of tomorrow's bread given today.

In the life of Hezekiah, as in the life of Jesus, are salvation and victory over sin and death. And when Jesus Christ has brought all the nations to himself, just as in Hezekiah's day, the thing will come about suddenly. On that glorious day we will receive the perfect peace that awaits those who put their trust in God. And while we wait? We give. We give.

21–27 July

4 God's weaker vessel, the woman with tender eyes

Genesis 29

One of the delights of the Bible is the abundance of its irony, its principle of proportion. God positions various contrasting elements within the redemptive story next to one another, highlighting his own attributes and through them, the subversive power of the gospel.

Among the Bible's most profound, most beautiful uses of this technique is its references to *weakness*. In Genesis 29:17, we learn this curious detail about the wife Jacob didn't want and was tricked into marrying: 'Leah's eyes were *weak*.' Some translations consider the Hebrew word here to mean 'tender' rather than weak, and rabbis teach this tenderness as caused by weeping due to much suffering. Leah is a wounded spirit.

God has introduced this tenderness before, in the story of three mysterious men who appear before Abraham. In keeping with a spirit of hospitality, 'Abraham also ran to the herd, and took a *tender* and choice calf and gave *it* to the servant, and he hurried to prepare it' (Genesis 18:7). God gives us more in David's words about his 'young and tender' son Solomon (1 Chronicles 22:5), the king who would build a temple to the Lord.

This messianic anticipation builds as we move on to where God multiples hope through the prophet Ezekiel to God's people in exile. Here again, God chooses the image of tenderness to draw our eye to he who would take on weakness, that tender sprig of cedar, planted on a high and lofty mountain (see Ezekiel 17:22–24).

Here is God's foolishness on display, wiser than human wisdom, stronger than human strength, bringing peace and rest greater than Solomon. He brings down the high tree and exalts the low tree. He dries up the green tree and makes the dry tree flourish. He is the Lord. He has spoken. He will perform it.

What mystery! In this heavenly helplessness is an irony that the kingdom of this world cannot comprehend, nor can it grasp after by its own hands. For God chooses the soft things of this world to break the solid. From among the wise he favours the foolish. To confound those who are mighty, he gives grace to the weak. He bestows his honour on the weaker vessel and raises the lowly to exaltation. All this we see in Leah, the woman with tender eyes, whom God saw was unloved. Whom he blessed.

5 Even the women and children rejoiced

Nehemiah 12:27–43; Ezekiel 8:14–15

In Ezekiel 8, the Spirit lifts Ezekiel between earth and heaven and brings him in the visions of God to Jerusalem, to the entrance of the north gate of the inner court, where the seat of the idol of jealousy is located. There, Ezekiel witnesses women sitting and weeping for Tammuz, an ancient Mesopotamian god believed to be a beautiful shepherd slain by a wild boar.

This is misplaced mourning. The image of the grieving woman in the Bible is a powerful one – and not to be trifled with.

Job evokes this intensity when he says, 'This is the portion of a wicked man from God… Though his sons are many, they are destined for the sword… Their widows will not be able to weep.' (Job 27:13–15). Jesus later reminds a crowd of mourning women of this: 'Daughters of Jerusalem, stop weeping for me, but weep for yourselves and for your children.' (Luke 23:28).

Recall that in Genesis 35, a boy with two names is born. On her deathbed, his mother Rachel gives her son his first name, *Ben-Oni, son of sorrows*. Rachel's burial place outside of Bethlehem cements her sorrow.

In this same place, Nebuchadnezzar would later assemble the people of Judah for their long trek into Babylonian captivity. Then, as the prophet Jeremiah grieves with and over his people in exile, he uses the image of their mother Rachel, who wept over her newborn baby.

This divine demonstration heralds God's own sorrow over those who weary themselves committing injustice. *And when God grieves, women are often his mouthpiece.* As Jeremiah is overcome with sadness, God tells him to send for the mourning women and tell them to teach their daughters how to grieve. Only when women of God weep can all God's people's eyes shed tears and our eyelids flow with water (Jeremiah 9:17–18).

And only when women of God rejoice has genuine peace arrived, as when Nehemiah appoints two great choirs to stand with him in the house of God. 'Even the women and children rejoiced' (Nehemiah 12:43).

This is more than a vision of God's people returning from Babylonian exile. It is a picture of a new heaven and earth, where all of God's children, the Bride of Jesus Christ will sing. Strength and honour are our clothing. We will rejoice in time to come.

6 The song of the Lamb

2 Chronicles 20:1–23; Luke 24:5–7

When Jehoshaphat, King of Judah, was outnumbered on the battlefield, he prayed to the Lord for help, and the Lord answered him with hope through Jahaziel, son of Zechariah. *You need not fight. The Lord is with you.* In response, the king bowed with his face to the ground, together with all of Judah. And on that night before battle, the Levites stood up and praised the Lord with a loud voice (see Matthew 26:30).

On the next day, they rose early in the morning and went out to the wilderness of Tekoa. There, as they turned their faces towards the battle, Jehoshaphat put *not soldiers but singers* before their enemies. And when these holy singers began singing and praising, the Lord turned Judah's songless enemies against one another, and 'they helped to destroy one another' (2 Chronicles 20:23) till no one escaped.

Victory completed, God's enemy defeated, the people of Judah went down to collect the spoil. There was so much, God tells us, that they were *three days* taking the spoil, more than they could carry. So weighed down with God's abundant gifts, on the fourth day, Judah assembled and named that place Valley of Beracah, 'Valley of Blessings'. And they returned to Jerusalem in peace with joy, carrying their instruments.

When God created the world, the angels sang over what he had made (Job 38:7). God himself rejoices over us with singing (Hebrews 2:11–13). Made in God's image, by God's loving hand, we return to him his Song of Songs (James 5:13).

And as we sing, we stand still and see the salvation of God over all the evil one and all his forces. These enemies we have seen, we will 'never see them again forever' (Exodus 14:13–14). For the Lord our God is in our midst. The Mighty One will save. He will quiet us with his love (Zephaniah 3:17). He will carry us in peace through the valley of this violent world, to the New Jerusalem, City of God.

Guidelines

A tolerance and even hunger for violence has captivated much of the Christian church in the western world. As Bethlehem Pastor Isaac Munther rebuked us in Christmas 2023:

> *Here in Palestine the Bible is weaponised against us. Our very own sacred text. In our terminology in Palestine, we speak of the empire. Here we confront the Theology of Empire, a disguise for superiority, supremacy, chosenness and entitlement. It is sometimes given a nice cover using words like 'Mission' and 'Evangelism', 'fulfilment of prophecy' and 'spreading freedom and liberty'. It speaks of land without people.*

I. Munther, 'Jesus under the rubble in Gaza': Bethlehem Pastor Isaac's impassioned plea for ceasefire (2023). Available at **youtube.com/watch?v=PwHr_vmW-oo**

The first week of notes in this series intended to draw attention to the absurdity of all human warfare; this second week of notes has focused on the grief and restlessness that all earthly empires inflict, in tension with the hope for peace and justice God offers us both today and in the life to come.

In response, this week's challenge to all readers is to *refocus* our minds and hearts on the perfect justice, truth and peace of God, which unsettles and dismantles all earthly empire. This salvation of the whole world God accomplishes, not using the weapons of the oppressor but rather a divine armour that appears without apology as weakness to the world and its powers.

With all your heart this week, as Jesus Christ did in his ministry on earth, remember who you are. We bring good news to the poor, comfort to those whose hearts and bodies are broken. We tell the captives they are free, the prisoners that they are released. And lest your words be little more than empty, future-focused promises, remember that the kingdom of Jesus Christ is one of radical equality and the love that fuels it. There is no love in war. There can be no war in love.

FURTHER READING

A. Bishara, 'Palestinian Christian Networked Activism: Reifying "Nonviolence" or Divining Justice?' in *Review of Middle East Studies*, vol. 43. no. 2 (2009), pp. 178-188.

J. Dear, 'Nonviolence Is Christian Love in Action: A Conversation with John Lewis', Center for Action and Contemplation (15 November 2022): **cac.org/news/nonviolence-is-christian-love-in-action-a-conversation-with-john-lewis**

'Global Peacemakers Speak', Bethlehem Bible College: **bipj.org/resources**

Hosea

Miriam Bier Hinksman

The superscription to the book of Hosea places the prophet Hosea in eighth-century BC Israel under King Jeroboam (1:1). The major feature of this context was the growing threat of Assyria, which would go on to destroy Israel in 722 BC. Hosea may not have witnessed this event himself, but he certainly anticipated it, and interpreted the impending Assyrian invasion as God's judgement upon Israel for abandoning their covenant loyalty to God. Hosea's prophetic vocation was to call the people of Israel back to their first love, warning them to remember this covenant relationship before they were destroyed.

There are three main sections in Hosea: Hosea 1:1—3:5; 4:1—11:11; and 11:12—14:9. Chapters 1—3 hinge on the story of Hosea taking a 'wife of whoredom' and having 'children of whoredom'. Images taken from female fertility, as well as the fertility of the natural world, continue throughout the book. The middle section interweaves announcements of judgement with heartfelt pleas for Israel to return to God, as God seemingly deliberates about Israel's fate – destruction or restoration. Chapters 12—14 continue in a similar vein, appealing to the history of Israel's relationship with God to explain the state they have got themselves into, before concluding with a hopeful vision of a possible future.

These notes highlight selected key passages from Hosea. There is much that cannot be covered here, and so as a 'next step' I suggest my Grove book, *Reading Hosea: A beginner's guide*. This offers further background and detail and a more extensive reading list.

Please note that these comments (like the book of Hosea) cover potentially sensitive material, including mentioning prostitution, adultery and the inability to have children.

Unless otherwise stated, Bible quotations are taken from the NRSV.

1 A fertile woman and a family metaphor

Hosea 1:2—2:1

Within the first few verses, the book of Hosea presents us with a prophet marrying a prostitute – a strange, and possibly offensive, idea. Hosea is called to 'Go, take for yourself a wife of whoredom and have children of whoredom, for the land commits great whoredom by forsaking the Lord' (v. 2). In other words, the people of Israel have strayed so far from the covenant relationship that they are like a woman who has sex with many men, instead of being faithful to the marriage bond.

Likening the relationship between God and God's people to a marriage was a startling innovation at the time. This illustration has had a vivid afterlife, both within and beyond the Bible, and has come to be known as the 'marriage metaphor'. As Hosea 1 proceeds, however, we are introduced not only to Hosea's wife, Gomer, but also to her children: Jezreel, Lo-Ammi and Lo-Ruhamah. It would be more apt, therefore, to call this a 'family metaphor', as Hosea's whole family is involved in performing the prophetic word to Israel (see further Alice Keefe, *Woman's Body and the Social Body in Hosea 1–2*, London, Sheffield Academic, 2001, p. 15).

Gomer's children have significant names, carrying the meaning of the prophetic word to Israel. Jezreel was a place of battle. Lo-Ammi means 'Not my people' and Lo-Ruhamah means 'Not-pitied'. To our ears, this can sound a little harsh. Through no fault of their own, these children are given unusual and unpleasant names to fulfil Hosea's vocation of bringing God's word of judgement to the people of Israel.

By the end of the chapter, however, something has changed. The word of judgement embedded in the children's names has become the promise of salvation, and their names are reframed accordingly. Jezreel may have been a place of battle, but it is also a fertile place. So too will Israel flourish, grow and be fruitful in the land. Instead of 'not my people', Lo-Ammi will be renamed Ammi, 'my people', and the people of Israel will once more be called 'children of the living God'. And God will again take pity on the people of Israel, renaming Lo-Ruhamah to reflect this: she will be called Ruhamah. Thus the prophet, his wife *and* their children, perform the prophetic word to Israel.

2 A fertile land and a fertile woman laid waste

Hosea 2:2–13

Sometimes we are so focused on what the Bible has to say to us (human beings) that we miss what it has to say about the rest of creation. But in prophetic thinking, the human and non-human worlds cannot be separated. Land and people operate in symbiotic relationship: if something affects the people of Israel, it will also affect her land, and vice versa. Contrast the way many people in cities these days are so far removed from the natural world that some children, when asked, will say that milk comes from supermarkets.

In Hosea 2, the fertile land and people of Israel are figured as a fertile wife and mother. What happens to the land happens to the people, and vice versa; and both are represented by what happens to this metaphorical woman. She has enjoyed the attentions of her lovers: the foreign nations and/or idols to which Israel turns for security, instead of turning to God. She assumes that the rich grain, wine and oil she enjoys (the fruits of the fertile land) come from these lovers, as her pay. She has not realised that all good things come from God – in the metaphor, her husband.

Her punishment is to be stripped naked, as a picture of the way in which the fruitful harvests of grain, wine and oil will be stripped away from Israel. She is stripped of her wool and flax clothing and left exposed in the wilderness, as a picture of the way in which the land and people of Israel will be ravaged. Finally, her cultivated vineyards and fig trees are laid waste, becoming an untamed forest full of wild animals, as a picture of the way in which Israel will be laid waste and left desolate.

We must understand that this chapter no longer concerns Hosea's wife Gomer, or any other real woman. Rather, the image of a woman stripped naked and left exposed in the desert to die is employed to say something about the land and its inhabitants, and their relationship with God. It is a metaphor; a devastating picture of punishment for forgetting God. But, as in chapter 1, at the end of the chapter something changes. There is a promise of future salvation for both the people and land of Israel – once again represented by the image of a woman. We will look at this in the next section.

3 Fertility restored, fertility denied

Hosea 2:14—3:5

In the previous section we saw how Hosea 2 pictures judgement upon Israel as a woman stripped and left without food or water to die in the wilderness. This symbolises the way in which Hosea foresees the land and people of Israel being devastated by the impending Assyrian invasion.

But the chapter holds the possibility of a future salvation, also pictured by a woman in the wilderness. Now, instead of a place of punishment, the wilderness is a place of romance. The early days of God's special relationship with Israel, when God brought her out of Egypt, are remembered (in perhaps a more positive light than they were experienced at the time!). The wilderness is reimagined as a place of renewed and restored relationship.

Just as judgement encompasses both the land and people of Israel, so does the hope of God's mercy. God's renewed covenant with Israel will be for her animals, birds and all the creeping things of the ground, not just for her people (v. 18). If Israel will return to her husband, then all her inhabitants, human and non-human, will have rest in the land (v. 18). Instead of a barren wilderness, there will be cultivated vineyards, as Israel is 'sown' in the land (v. 23). God's promise for Israel is that he will take her as his 'wife forever', in 'righteousness and in justice, in steadfast love, and in mercy', 'in faithfulness', and that she shall 'know the Lord' (vv. 19–20).

In the final episode in the 'story' of Hosea's marriage (3:1–5) the prophet says to his wife: 'You must remain as mine for many days; you shall not play the whore, you shall not have intercourse with a man, *nor I with you*' (v. 3, my italics). There is still an element of punishment here, in the withholding of sexual relations. Without sexual relations, there can be no children – no fertility or fruitfulness in the land. The woman's capacity for sexual reproduction, now denied, illustrates the way in which Israel would, for a time, be denied both the royal and religious leaders who were supposed to be the guarantors of her relationship with God and thus of her safety and flourishing in the land. Only when the Israelites 'return and seek the Lord their God' will they 'come in awe to the Lord and to his goodness' (v. 5).

4 It takes two to tango

Hosea 4

Images of women, their bodies and their reproductive capacity appear throughout Hosea. Sometimes these images are used metaphorically; sometimes they may refer to real women in eighth-century BC Israel. We know Gomer's name, but there are also glimpses of other women, and the effect God's judgement upon Israel will have upon them. So now we ask the question – what about the real women of Israel?

In chapter 4, there is a shift from talking about metaphorical whoredom to talking about women who *actually* 'play the whore' (v. 13). Curiously, having just pictured the nation of Israel's sin as a sexually promiscuous woman who will be thoroughly punished, Hosea 4 states that when the daughters and daughters-in-law of Israel play the whore and commit adultery, they will *not* be punished (vv. 13–14). Why? Because it is 'the men themselves [who] go aside with whores' (4:14). There is recognition here of a dynamic that is often overlooked in contemporary discussions of prostitution and morality: prostitution only exists because men seek out sex for hire.

For Hosea, then, the women of Israel are not to blame when they 'play the whore' and 'commit adultery'. Rather, responsibility lies with the men who seek them out. This is an important corrective when you consider that in the previous three chapters, Israel's sins were writ large on the body of a woman. Even when the woman's body is being used metaphorically, as a cipher for the land and people of Israel, there can be a temptation to collapse the metaphor into the idea that *actual* women are somehow to blame for Israel's situation – a situation so serious that God's judgement is looming. But Hosea is clear who he holds responsible: the greedy priests, who operate the sacrificial system for their own gain rather than for the atonement of the people's sins; and the blind prophets, who have neglected their duty to make God known (vv. 4–10). If the people of Israel are 'destroyed for lack of knowledge' and have 'forgotten the law', it is because these religious leaders are not doing their job. Hosea 4 reminds us that although Israel has been figured as a woman, it is the male leaders of Israel who have led the people astray. It is the 'men themselves' who 'go aside with whores'.

5 How can I give you up? God's changing mind

Hosea 11:1–11

The opening chapters of Hosea moved from messages of judgement to messages of salvation, communicated both in the names of Gomer's children and in the image of the woman in the wilderness. The conflict between judgement and salvation continues throughout Hosea and can be seen as a conflict within God's own self – a conflict between God's justice and God's mercy. At one moment, God seems intent on punishing Israel for their covenant failures and unfaithfulness. The next, God appears anguished at the thought of losing the beloved Israel and determines to have compassion upon them.

Nowhere is this conflict more pronounced than in Hosea 11, where we are given an almost inside view of the debate going on within God's own self. The chapter now presents us with a different metaphor: the picture of God the loving parent and Israel the rebellious son (vv. 1–4). This picture of God as a parent is one of the best known and loved parts of Hosea, and for good reason. It speaks of God's love for Israel, despite their faithlessness from almost the very beginning (v. 2). It uses familiar scenes from family life to illustrate the way in which God has loved and cared for Israel as one would love and care for a small child – teaching them to walk, scooping them up for a hug, leading them kindly, lifting them up, leaning down to them, and feeding them (vv. 3–4).

But while the chapter begins with this affecting portrait of Israel in his infancy, being nurtured by a God who dotes upon him, a few verses later it seems that God has decided to give Israel over to his enemies 'because they have refused to return to me' (v. 5). In almost the next breath, God is agonising over whether it is really possible to give up on Israel, recoiling at the very idea (v. 8).

This movement from love, to anger, to renewed compassion, suggests that in this moment, the 'jury is still out' on whether God will execute judgement upon Israel for their covenant failures, or whether God will relent and have mercy, gathering in the children of Israel from every direction to bring them home again (vv. 10–11).

6 A lush and fertile land

Hosea 14

While much of Hosea is written in the minor key, emphasising God's imminent judgement, the 'last word' in each section is always a word of hope and salvation. The final chapter of Hosea amplifies this hopeful outlook. Hosea 14 entreats Israel to return to God, confessing their sin and determining to trust only in God. It then presents one last vision of a possible future. Israel is pictured as a lush and fertile garden, filled with spreading shoots, beautiful olive trees and fragrant plants. God's own self will be like a cypress tree – evergreen, ever faithful, and providing the shelter and shade that Israel needs to grow and flourish. It is a beautiful vision, equating a flourishing future for the people of Israel with a lush and fertile land.

Hosea's prophetic vocation was to call Israel back to a loving and faithful relationship with God. If they had listened, perhaps this vision could have become a reality. Instead, the kingdom of Israel was destroyed by Assyria in 722BC. If it was too late for Israel, then why do we still have these words?

Prophetic words can speak into many different situations. Hosea's original horizon was the eighth-century kingdom of Israel, but throughout the book there are mentions of Judah – perhaps from a different pen – suggesting that Hosea's words may also be relevant to them. The kingdom of Judah survived when Israel did not, but almost two centuries later they faced their own threat of destruction at the hands of the Babylonians. It is as if someone has recalled Hosea's warnings to Israel, and applied them, years later, to Judah.

Our own time is yet another horizon into which Hosea's words might speak. The closing words of Hosea are a Proverbs-like injunction to all who are wise and discerning to take heed and 'understand these things'. It can be a challenge to apply ancient words to contemporary contexts, but there are certainly aspects of Hosea's message to Israel that stand the test of time. We might not choose the image of an unfaithful wife to speak of our own failures and faithlessness, but we can still hear the call to seek a relationship with God that is characterised by righteousness, justice, steadfast love, mercy and the knowledge of God (cf. 3:19–20).

Guidelines

Gomer and her children play key roles in Hosea's prophetic word to Israel – willingly or otherwise. Can you think of other roles where a whole family is affected by the vocation of one of its members? (Perhaps you have had the experience of being a 'clergy kid' or a 'military brat'.) How might this affect a child growing up in such a family?

Names often have significant meanings. Gomer's children were given names expressing God's judgement upon Israel, and then their names were reframed to express the hope of salvation. What name would *you* choose, if you could rename yourself to express your own experience of God's salvation?

Hosea uses many different images and metaphors to characterise the relationship between God and Israel. We have focused on two of them – the so-called marriage metaphor, and the parent-child metaphor. What other metaphors can you think of for the relationship between God and God's people? Is there one that particularly draws you? Are you able to identify why?

Hosea's prophetic vocation was to call Israel back to their 'first love' of God. Because of failures of leadership, the people of Israel had forgotten what it was to know God – to really *know* God, rather than performing their religious duties out of obligation at best, and self-interested gain at worst. Does your relationship with God feel like duty or joy? Are you compelled by a fear of punishment, or drawn by a delight in the intimacy of knowing and loving God?

In Christian theology, the doctrine of the impassibility of God is the idea that God does not suffer or feel emotion and cannot be changed by anything outside of Godself. How might Hosea 11 enter into conversation with this doctrine?

Hosea ends with an injunction for the wise to 'understand these things'. How do you think Hosea could be applied today? Are there limits to the extent to which ancient prophetic words can be applied to contemporary contexts?

FURTHER READING

Paula Gooder, *Hosea to Micah: A Bible commentary for every day* (BRF Ministries, 2005).

Miriam Bier Hinksman, *Reading Hosea: A beginner's guide* (Grove Books, 2023).

Teachable moments: discipling on the way in Luke's gospel

George Wieland

When and where has your most significant learning taken place? Most of us have benefited from formal classroom learning and study programmes, but have you also been surprised by new realisations and shifting perspectives in unexpected times and places? Some years ago, educational theorist Robert Havighurst observed that for learning to be effective it must be delivered in a 'teachable moment' when the learner is personally engaged and open to new understanding (*Human Development and Education*, Longmans, 1952). Such opportunities often fall outside the formal teaching environment. The skilled educator – or, in our context, discipler – looks for those 'teachable moments' when defensiveness is broken down and assumptions can be subverted.

That is how Jesus taught. Certainly, there were occasions when he spoke at length to various audiences in synagogues, the temple or other locations. For his disciples, however, learning often happened as they were on the road with Jesus. Interruptions, unplanned encounters, criticism, threats, awkward social situations – all became 'teachable moments' in which the disciples' understanding of Jesus and the kingdom of God was reshaped.

In Luke's gospel the motif of 'the way' is highly significant. It is 'the way of peace' (1:79), 'the way of the Lord' (3:4), 'the way of God' (20:21). Jesus' journey to Jerusalem (9:51—19:44), where his final confrontation with the authorities of temple, nation and empire would take place, provides a narrative framework for much of Jesus' teaching 'on the way'. In Luke's second volume, Acts, 'the way' represents the life and teaching of the Jesus community (Acts 9:2; 18:25–26; 19:9, 23; 24:14, 22). Over the next two weeks we shall accompany the disciples in some of those 'teachable moments' through which they were being formed for participation in the way of the kingdom.

Unless otherwise stated, Bible quotations are taken from the NRSV. Author references are to works in the 'further reading list' on page 123.

4–10 August

1 A lost child

Luke 2:40–52

This passage should come with a trigger warning! Anyone who has ever been responsible for looking after children on a trip will feel something of the anxiety, fear and guilt that must have seized Mary and Joseph when it dawned on them that their twelve-year-old son was missing. They had already been on the road for a full day, returning to Nazareth with other local families after observing the Passover in Jerusalem. There was no option, however, but to retrace their steps and search the streets of the city for any trace of Jesus. Finally, after three days of growing panic, there he was: in the temple, deep in discussion with Israel's foremost religious scholars. Imagine the mix of relief and anger, hurt and joy, as well as bewilderment. Why was he there, and what was he doing? From the perspective of the anxious parents, why had he put them through this ordeal? That was a teachable moment!

Luke's framing of this episode is significant. It is bracketed by two statements affirming Jesus' growth in wisdom, maturity and favour with God and other people (vv. 40, 52). However Mary and Joseph might have seen it at the time, this is what wisdom and God's approval looks like. In those first words that Jesus speaks in Luke's gospel, the child disciples his parents. Although he does return with Mary and Joseph to their home, he affirms that he belongs by right in God his Father's house (v. 49). He is governed now by divine necessity, indicated by the Greek term *dei*, 'must', not only in those few days in Jerusalem but throughout his life and ministry (v. 49; compare 4:43; 9:22; 17:25; 19:5; 22:37; 24:7, 26, 44).

Glimpses of truth received in teachable moments may take time to come fully into focus. Mary was still perplexed, but she never forgot what her son began to teach her in that time and place (v. 51). As the gospel story unfolds, she and we, Luke's readers, will be challenged again to recognise that our primary family relationship is with God, Jesus' Father and ours (8:19–21). We shall also discover that it is sometimes children who are the teachers from whom adults must learn the way of the kingdom (9:46–48; 18:15–17).

2 Jesus shows up at work

Luke 5:1–11

Simon had evidently known Jesus before the incident recorded here. In the arrangement of Luke's narrative (where admittedly thematic ordering often trumps strict chronology), Jesus had already been a guest in Simon's house, where he had healed Simon's mother-in-law (4:38–39). Jesus' choice of Simon's boat to teach from (v. 3) and Simon's use of the term *epistatēs* (master) to address Jesus (v. 5) both suggest an existing relationship. In this episode, however, that relationship moves on to another level.

The kind of fishing that Simon and his business partners earned their living from was done at night, when the nets were invisible to the fish. That particular night had been depressingly unproductive. Coming back to shore in the early morning with nothing to show for their hard work, all they could do was set about preparing the nets for the next night's attempt. But they were interrupted. Jesus was there, a crowd swarming around him, hungry for his teaching. Seeing that a couple of boats had come in, one of them Simon's, Jesus climbed in and asked for a favour: 'Would you mind pushing out a little from the shore? I'll be heard better from there.'

We're not told what the fishermen thought of that, when they just wanted to sort their nets out and head home, but there does seem to be some exasperation in Simon's response to Jesus' next request, that they go back out onto the lake and try again. Why should professional fishermen take instructions from a carpenter about how to do their job? But they did it, and the result was staggering: an unimaginable, miraculous catch. Now Jesus certainly had their attention. They had front-row seats as Jesus taught the crowd, but none of that is preserved. The teachable moment for them came when Jesus entered their own work context and startled them with an awe-inspiring demonstration of divine power in a way that spoke specifically to them. Now, they saw him – and themselves – differently, and when Jesus announced that their lives were to take a radically different direction in which all their skills and qualities would be utilised in participation in his work, they were ready to leave their boats and follow him. They had learned that whatever challenges lay ahead, they could face them by doing what Jesus said.

3 Disapproval

Luke 5:27–39

Most of us prefer the warm glow of approval to the sharp sting of disapproval, particularly when it comes from people regarded as guardians of the community's values. The disciples soon discovered that if they were to go around with Jesus, criticism from the learned and powerful would be an uncomfortably common experience. Today's reading recounts the first of several meal scenes involving Jesus in Luke's gospel. Culturally, the sharing of food was an enactment of relationship: shared meals meant shared lives, implying mutual acceptance. That was why the presence of Jesus at an extravagant banquet hosted by a tax collector for his equally unsavoury friends caused such consternation. How could someone who spoke and acted as a God-anointed prophet associate with people who, by standard criteria, were disqualified from inclusion among God's holy people? Jesus was the guest of honour, completely at home in that environment, but what about the disciples? Did they have any misgivings about following Jesus into a gathering of people derided as 'tax collectors and sinners'? Apart from any religious qualms, it seems unlikely that Galilean small-business owners would have been warmly disposed towards the local enforcer of a corrupt taxation system.

It was, however, to the disciples that the criticism was directed: 'Why do you eat and drink with tax collectors and sinners?' (v. 30) They might have been wondering themselves how they had got into that situation! But Jesus chose that teachable moment of uncertainty and vulnerability to articulate – for them as well as for the critics – the nature and scope of his mission: to seek out and restore those in need of healing and forgiveness, and to gather them into the joyful, abundant life of God's kingdom. The mission of Jesus and his disciples could only be accomplished as they entered into real relationship with those who seemed currently to be outside that kingdom.

The next complaint was that Jesus' disciples just seemed to be having far too much fun for people supposed to be serious about their religious commitment (v. 33)! In response, Jesus turned the criticism of apparent rule-breaking into a critique of the rule-keeping mentality. The way of Jesus is radically new, and the old forms cannot accommodate it, neither as a top-up nor an add-on. The disciples' rule of life must conform to the nature of the kingdom, not the other way round.

4 Scandal

Luke 7:36–50

Earlier in this chapter we are told that Jesus and a crowd of followers had gone to a town called Nain (v. 11), and it seems that Jesus stayed there until he commenced another preaching tour (8:1). If so, Simon the Pharisee was a resident of Nain and his dinner invitation followed closely after Jesus restored a dead man to life (vv. 11–17) and reassured messengers from John the Baptist that he was indeed the one they were waiting for (vv. 18–35). The talk in the town was that 'a great prophet has risen among us' (v. 16). Simon was evidently not convinced. Despite inviting Jesus to a meal, he had blatantly failed to treat him as an honoured guest: no water to wash his feet, no kiss of greeting, no oil for his head (vv. 44–46). Jesus was there because Simon wanted to evaluate this so-called prophet for himself. And as far as he was concerned, when Jesus did not even have the discernment to rebuff the indecent attentions of a well-known 'sinner' who had gate-crashed the dinner party, the question was settled: this was no prophet (v. 39).

It is not stated explicitly that the disciples were with Jesus in the house, but whether they observed the scene first-hand or had it related to them, we can imagine them cringing with embarrassment. First, as the woman appeared at the Pharisee's table and approached – of all people – their master, Jesus, in a scandalous display of intimacy and affection; and then as they anticipated the reaction of the distinguished host. For the disciples as well as for Simon, this was a teachable moment.

Jesus seized the initiative, addressing Simon directly. First, a parable, eliciting the Pharisee's agreement that someone who had been released from a huge burden of debt might be expected to love the one who had set them free. And then, the turning point: 'Do you see this woman?' (v. 44). Simon had certainly seen her, as had everyone else. He had seen a 'sinner' behaving disgracefully, threatening the purity of his home and his own reputation. But Jesus had seen her love, faith and gratitude, and he welcomed from her the loving service and honour that Simon had withheld. If the disciples were to do as Jesus did, they must learn to see as Jesus saw.

4–10 August

5 An impossible task

Luke 9:10–17

This is one of very few episodes in Jesus' ministry to be recorded in all four gospels. It must often have been told and retold among the earliest believers. A distinctive feature of Luke's account is that he specifies that it was 'the twelve' who urged Jesus to 'send the crowd away' (v. 12). Just a few verses earlier, Jesus had sent the twelve out, empowered to participate in his ministry, trusting God to provide for their needs (vv. 1–3). They had plenty to report when they returned (v. 10), but their performance in this ensuing scene suggests that there was still more to learn about the way and the power of Jesus. To be fair, the situation was challenging beyond anything they might have experienced before. There were literally thousands of hungry people, and time was running out for them to arrange food for themselves. The twelve apostles perhaps felt that it was up to them in their recently acquired status to intervene. Their wonderful but sometimes otherworldly leader seemed to be unaware of the impending crisis. How could they provide food in the wilderness?

Jesus did not thank them for their timely warning. Instead, he directed the challenge back to them: 'You give them something to eat' (v. 13). That was clearly impossible; they were being set up to fail. Incomprehension, panic, anger… a teachable moment! And we know what happened. Jesus did feed the crowd, but as he did so, he was discipling the apostles. Both in the moment and as they continued to reflect on it, they were learning about the identity and compassion of Jesus and how to share in his ministry. In Jesus they were glimpsing the God of Israel who had indeed spread a table in the wilderness (Psalm 78:19–20). As Jesus looked up to heaven, invoked blessing, and the creative power of God flowed through his hands to generate all that was needed, their faith grew. In the experience of participating in this miraculous provision they were given a pattern for their own ministry: first, place the little that they have in Jesus' hands; then receive it back from Jesus; and carry to others what they have received from his hands.

Notice the recurrence of that number 'twelve' (v. 17). Twelve baskets of food left over – one each! In serving others, their own needs were also met.

6 Wrong again!

Luke 9:43–56

Just how wrong is it possible to be? In today's reading the disciples repeatedly get it wrong. They were wrong about Jesus: they could not comprehend how the one whom they had been following and observing, through whom the greatness of God was manifested in remarkable ways, would be overpowered by mere human hands (vv. 44–45). They were wrong about status: still convinced that they were on the way with Jesus to a glorious victory, their thoughts turned to how the anticipated honour and power would be distributed, and who would have the highest status (v. 46). They were wrong about boundaries: concern for their own recognition went hand in hand with indignation that anyone outside their privileged group should dare to perform works of power in Jesus' name (v. 49). Perhaps it stung more sharply because whoever that person was, he had evidently succeeded in an area of ministry where the disciples had failed (v. 40). They were wrong about power: when the residents of a Samaritan village refused the disciples' request for hospitality on their journey, James and John wanted to do for their prophet, Jesus, what the great prophet Elijah had done, calling down fire in judgement on a Samaritan king who had refused to acknowledge the God of Israel (v. 54; see 2 Kings 1:1–16).

Four serious mistakes, but each of them served as a teachable moment. Luke underlines the failure of the disciples to grasp what they were hearing from Jesus about the necessity that he should suffer. 'They did not understand… its meaning remained concealed from them… they could not perceive it… they were afraid to ask' (v. 45). As time after time their responses exposed mistaken assumptions and misdirected concerns, Jesus responded with rebukes that brought them up short and, one nudge at a time, began to reorient them from their vision of human victory, status, privilege and power towards a new imagination of a completely upside-down kingdom. In the way of Jesus, victory comes through self-giving (v. 44), human measures of status are subverted (v. 48), boundaries, even those of the inner group of Jesus' closest disciples, must not be deployed to limit the mediation of Jesus' ministry of release (v. 50), and the way of Jesus' kingdom is not one of coercion but one of humility and peace (vv. 55–56).

4–10 August

Guidelines

- 'What Jesus is doing is putting into effect the new world that God is bringing about – and the old ways just don't fit' (Wright, 63). What teachable moments have you experienced that have pointed you towards the character of the new world under the rule of Jesus?
- For the disciples, many teachable moments occurred when they were with Jesus in the company of people regarded as impure and irreligious. What opportunities do you have to follow Jesus into such company? Have there been teachable moments for you on such occasions? Are there times when concern for your reputation or perceived purity have kept you apart from people to whom Jesus wants to bring wholeness of life?
- For many churches and Christians, mission includes inviting people into our space, whether that be organising events at church or hosting people in our homes. In Luke's gospel, both Jesus and his disciples were more often guests than hosts. Reflect on some of the meal scenes in Luke and consider what it would involve for you or your church to engage your community as guests instead of hosts.

11–17 August

1 Pre-trip anxiety

Luke 10:1–16

You're about to set out on a trip. Your heart rate rises, your mind is flooded with things that you need to think about, but you just can't focus. Have you forgotten anything? Are you sure about the itinerary? What will you do if your plans don't work out? Are you ready for this? Should you even be going? You are experiencing a very common phenomenon: pre-trip anxiety. It may be unpleasant, but it is a teachable moment. The mission trip leader gathering the group into a huddle at the airport while they wait to board, like a sports coach giving the changing-room talk as the team prepares to walk out onto the field, knows that what they say in that moment of heightened receptivity could be crucial. People respond to anxiety in different ways. Some demand highly detailed instructions – what to do, what to say, how to respond in a range of situations. Others need to see the big picture within which to comprehend the nature and purpose of what they are being sent out to do. Some have to be reassured that their participation matters.

In Jesus' pre-trip team talk, he sent the disciples out with clear instructions and an understanding of the nature and significance of what they were to do. In effect, they were to represent Jesus wherever they went, knowing that Jesus himself was on his way. They were to offer peace, enact liberation and declare the presence of the kingdom. The mission was urgent. Jesus was on his way to Jerusalem and they were in a harvest season of limited duration. It required a suspension of normal life while the opportunity was seized. They were to go as 'lambs into the midst of wolves' (v. 3), not amply resourced but vulnerable, not setting themselves up as hosts but arriving as needy guests, dependent on the hospitality of the people to whom they went. They were to go humbly, accepting whatever they were given rather than scouting around for a better option. They were agents of a peaceable kingdom, glad to find people of peace who would become partners, but aware that they might be rejected. Such rejection might feel like failure, but they were not sales reps, charged with closing the deal; the success of their mission would lie in how authentically they represented Jesus and embodied his kingdom.

2 The debrief

Luke 10:17–24

And now they're back, brimming over with excitement, eager to share all that they have experienced. For Jesus, this was another teachable moment.

First, he helped them to interpret their experience theologically. They couldn't wait to relate the exhilarating stories of seeing demons brought under control through their ministry (v. 17). Jesus gently lifted their eyes from what they were tempted to regard as their own power to a larger, cosmic reality. The submission of demonic powers to the name of Jesus was an instance of the defeat of Satan and the breaking in of the kingdom of God, redeeming the world from the stranglehold of evil (v. 18). Second, he encouraged them to recognise and own the competence that they did have, because Jesus' commissioning included the enabling to do what Jesus wanted them to do (v. 19). Third, Jesus gently interrogated their values. While they were intoxicated with what they had achieved, Jesus encouraged them to value who they were and to whom they belonged over what they had been able to do (v. 20). Identity will endure long beyond accomplishment.

Today's passage also relates Jesus' response as he listened to his disciples (vv. 21–23). There was immense joy in recognising the Father's handiwork in the disciples' growth. There was delight in seeing how the Father values and works in and through people that the world would not choose. A prayer of thanksgiving welled up in Jesus: 'Father, look what you've done – bypassed the obvious candidates for attaining deep spiritual knowledge and revealing all this to these people, my unimpressive followers! That is so like you, isn't it, taking the weak and the poor and making them agents of your reign and salvation!' That might have been humbling for the disciples who had just returned buoyed up with impressive stories to tell! But as they held on to those words through life, they would have been glad of the reassurance that spiritual success and insight were not their own achievement but the gracious gift of God.

To accompany others on their journeys of faith and service can be demanding, sometimes draining, with many disappointments. But the reward for disciplers, as for Jesus, can be deep joy in seeing God at work and a more profound appreciation of God's grace and power.

3 A heated family argument

Luke 10:38–42

A recurring theme in Jesus' journey towards Jerusalem is how he and his message were received. Here, two kinds of reception are contrasted. Martha's is expressed by the Greek term *hupodechomai* (v. 38). This has the sense of welcoming a guest into one's home, often with generous hospitality, as when Zacchaeus joyfully received Jesus to stay at his house (19:6). Martha evidently wanted to do the best that she could to entertain her honoured guest, and she got busy! She looked round for her sister, Mary, to help with the preparations, but she was nowhere to be found – at least, not in the spaces in the house where the women would conventionally remain while the men gathered in the main area. Shockingly, that's where Mary was! In among the men, right at the front, sitting at Jesus' feet. Why was Mary not playing her part in receiving Jesus in a worthy way? In fact, she was doing precisely that: she was 'listening to his word' (v. 39, NASB). The verb here is *akouō*, to hear, be attentive, obey. Those who 'hear the word of God and do it', said Jesus, are his true family (8:21). That was how Mary enacted her receptivity to Jesus and his message.

Suddenly, the calm scene in the room where Jesus was teaching was disrupted. A frustrated and angry sister burst into the room! Disregarding the rules of hospitality, she interrupted Jesus, rebuking him and demanding that he order her sister to share the work. That must have grabbed everyone's attention. A teachable moment! Jesus' response challenged conventional boundaries and gender roles. He welcomed Mary into his community of learners and followers along with all who would hear and obey his word, women and men, and, as we see elsewhere in Luke's gospel, Gentiles and Jews, children and adults, so-called 'sinners' as well as those regarded as righteous. Serving (*diakonia*, v. 40, a common term for 'ministry' in the New Testament) is necessary, but when it is distorted by anxiety and soured by resentment, it has lost sight of its goal and character. Martha assumed that her sister had been diverted from serving by listening to Jesus, but it was in fact Martha who had been distracted (Greek *perispaō*, 'drawn away,' v. 41) by what her serving had become from the one thing that was truly essential.

4 How do you do that?

Luke 11:1–13; 18:1–8

A young school chaplain whom I know recently helped out on a school camp. He had to check on the boys as they settled down for the first night. In the first tent he was surprised to be asked, 'Sir, could you teach us to pray?' The same request was repeated in the last tent that he visited. As far as he is aware, none of those boys have any Christian background or church connection. What had prompted their desire to pray? Being a non-religious school, the chaplain is asked not to overtly commend Christian belief, but at camp, he had been called upon to say grace before the evening meal. That seems to have been it! The boys had liked 'that grace' and thought it would be good to say a 'grace' at night, but didn't know how. They had heard the chaplain pray and wanted to be able to do that themselves.

In Luke's account, there is a similar teachable moment. Seeing their teacher praying (11:1) stirred in the disciples the desire to be able to pray, and Jesus seized the moment. In the narrative context of the journey to Jerusalem, the Lord's Prayer is a prayer for the road. It forms those who pray it as participants in the mission of Jesus. Terse as it is, it contains all that is needed. It begins in relationship: 'Father'; it continues with the primary goal of God's honour: 'May your name be revered as holy'; those who pray it align themselves with God's purpose for the world, being realised in Jesus: 'Your kingdom come'; they express dependence on God for daily provision, release for themselves and others from sin and indebtedness, and protection from whatever might draw them away from the life of faith and faithfulness.

To encourage them to take their requests to God, Jesus offers human comparisons. The friend who might do it grudgingly but can be persuaded to help (11:5–8); the parent, who, whatever their shortcomings, is unlikely to give something harmful to a hungry child (11:11–13); the judge (in a companion passage) who, corrupt as he is, will eventually enact justice if the plaintiff persists (18:1–8). In each case, the point is that if even such flawed people can be prevailed upon to grant requests, how much more may we trust God, the faithful friend, the loving parent, the just ruler.

5 A significant donation

Luke 20:45—21:4

Jesus had arrived in Jerusalem and was spending his days teaching in the temple. Increasingly, the kingdom that he embodied came into conflict with the economic, social and political elites who exploited the religious aspirations and practices of the people for their own status and wealth. Having spent time in debate with the scribes, the experts who interpreted the law and set the rules for the people to observe, Jesus turned away to speak very publicly about them (20:45). 'Beware of them,' he said, not only because they posed a threat to Jesus and his followers but also because their values and behaviour were not what Jesus wanted his disciples to adopt. The scribes sought high social status and the privileges that came with it. They demanded recognition, dressing in ways that signalled their importance and performing their religion in public in order to impress. Behind the scenes, however, they were utilising their legal expertise to leach money and property from widows, the most vulnerable people in society, leaving them impoverished and even homeless (20:46–47).

Just then, Jesus looked up, and there, in front of his eyes, the very things he had been talking about were being enacted. People were bringing their financial contributions to the temple. Whether placed in an open receptacle or handed to a priest, with a declaration of how much it was, it was not discreet! People of evident wealth were bringing sizeable donations, and in stark contrast a widow, at the other end of the economic scale, brought just two tiny coins (21:1). It was a teachable moment. What comprises a 'significant donation'? If we automatically think in terms of a large financial gift, it is chastening that Jesus relativised the contributions of the wealthy who continue to live in opulence while surrounded by poverty and saw greater worth in the sacrificial gift of the poor.

Yet in the context of what Jesus had been saying about the powerful and the widows (20:47), there is another challenge: why was she poor? Jesus condemned a religious system that benefitted the powerful while exploiting the very people for whom God cares deeply, and to whom Jesus brought good news (see Green, p. 728). We can both honour the costly devotion of the poor and share Jesus' anger at the social, economic and religious injustice that has impoverished them.

6 Grief

Luke 24:13–35

Grief: unbearable sadness, the stabbing pain of loss, hopes dashed, hurt and anger, mind and heart churning with questions and emotions. We would not choose grief, but it can be a teachable moment. So it proved for the two followers of Jesus as they trudged along the road to Emmaus, walking away from the intensity and upheaval of the past three days that had obliterated their hope, made nonsense of their faith and left them devastated.

Into that moment stepped Jesus, unrecognised. Why did he not immediately reveal his identity to reassure them that he was alive and restore their joy? He knew that they were not yet at the place where the reality of the risen Jesus could be grasped. Before talking, Jesus listened. He gave the grieving friends the opportunity to tell the story in their own way without jumping in to correct or elucidate. As they spoke, they were processing the experience, not only relating information but reaffirming who Jesus had been to them – 'a prophet mighty in deed and word' (v. 19) – naming their cruelly dashed hopes that he might have been their messiah. Eventually they conceded that there were unresolved questions, the puzzling absence of Jesus' body from the tomb, hints that he might even be alive… but no real evidence.

In that teachable moment, when their own understanding had been exhausted but they still longed for an explanation, Jesus supplied what was missing: a knowledge of the saving purpose of God expressed through scripture and the place of the Messiah in that story, making sense of his death and what was to follow. Their hearts burned! As they were drawn into the story of scripture, it came alive for them and opened up new possibilities.

Finally, the revelation was completed in another teachable moment. The mysterious companion on the road accepted their invitation to stay for a meal. Breaking convention, the guest assumed the role of the host. He took bread, blessed it, broke it, shared it with them… and their eyes were opened. At that point Jesus didn't need to say anything. He was simply there, activating the chain of teachable moments that he had built into the life of the community and that continues for us when he broke bread, poured out wine, and said, 'Do this in remembrance of me' (22:19).

Guidelines

- Who are you discipling, whether informally or in a more formal role? What are you learning from reflecting on Jesus' discipling 'on the way' about forming people for faith and faithfulness in the way of Jesus? How could you recognise and utilise teachable moments as you journey with them?
- Pause to thank God for the growth that you are privileged to see in others. Consider how to frame and build on their successes and help them to find learning in their experiences of failure.
- Reflect on Jesus' institution of the practice of communion as the provision of a perpetual chain of teachable moments. How might that aspect of its purpose be more fully appropriated, with openness to real encounter, fresh revelation and renewed perspective?

FURTHER READING

Paul Borgman, *The Way According to Luke: Hearing the whole story of Luke–Acts* (Eerdmans, 2006) – insightful study by a literary scholar of the theme of 'the way' through the two volumes of Luke's work.

Joel B. Green, *The Gospel of Luke (New International Commentary on the New Testament)* (Eerdmans, 1997) – thorough scholarly commentary taking a narrative approach to Luke's gospel.

Tom Wright, *Luke for Everyone* (SPCK, 2001) – informed by extensive scholarship but very accessible, offering information and insights on bite-sized sections of Luke's gospel.

A disabled reading of the healing miracles

Tanya Marlow

I am an occasional lecturer in pastoral theology. Whenever I meet a new group of trainee ministers, I ask them how they would preach one of the healing miracles, for example, the healing of the paralysed man or blind Bartimaeus. They outline their sermon with ease. Then I ask the crucial question, 'What if there's a wheelchair user or blind person in your congregation?' and I watch carefully as they squirm, realising that there are significant pastoral implications for the supposedly straightforward spiritual message.

How do we preach Jesus healing 'the deaf' when our Deaf congregant (who uses a capital D as a marker of identity and community) takes offence at the idea that deafness is a deficiency that needs correcting, rather than a beautiful gift? How do you explain the story of the immobile man at the pool of Bethesda whom Jesus warns about something worse happening to him, when facing you is a 13-year-old boy with Long Covid who now can't walk?

I have Myalgic Encephalomyelitis (M.E.), a devastating multi-system illness that has left me almost entirely bedbound for the last 15 years, though I can leave the house for a few hours in a wheelchair once a week or so. My ongoing, unhealed illness and suffering often makes other Christians uncomfortable. Even if a pastor doesn't believe that my sickness is caused by my sin or lack of belief, many church members do, and will tell me so. If this isn't addressed from the front, theologically, sadly the outcome is chronically ill people feeling forced from the church or the faith. As we study the gospels with fresh lenses, let's remember the pastoral and evangelistic importance of fine-tuning our understanding of disability and healing.

Unless otherwise stated, Bible quotations are taken from the NRSV.

18–24 August

1 Separating sin and sickness

Mark 2:1–12

Most disabled Christians have heard two things from the church at some point: first, that their condition is caused by their sin; second, that it is caused by their lack of faith. A careful reading of Mark 2 debunks both assumptions.

The phrase that strikes me in the first five verses is 'having dug through [the roof]' (v. 4). I have never seen a religious painting of this scene that shows debris falling on Jesus' head and the owners of the house pointing upwards in indignation as their property is damaged, yet that is surely what must have happened as the four people partially destroyed the roof so that Jesus could meet their friend. Mark's gospel plays with the contrast of *ochlos* (the crowd, where Jesus ministered) and *oikos* (the home, where Jesus gave more intimate revelations). Discontented to be part of the anonymous crowd, the paralysed man and his friends break rules and buildings in order to be seen by Jesus. Even today, disabled people often have to fight for full inclusion in churches, and buildings must be altered.

Jesus doesn't respond with indignation at their forced entry, but admiration for 'their faith' (v. 5) – carers and patient. Consider: if it is possible that Jesus heals people because of others' faith, presumably sick people can't be held responsible for their supposed lack thereof. Jesus compassionately calls the paralysed man *teknon*, 'child', or perhaps 'son', before declaring his sins forgiven.

Why, when someone's need was so obviously for healing, does Jesus focus on his sins (v. 5)? Some argue that this man's immobility was caused by sin, or that his sins were particularly awful; others assume that Jesus' priority is not for our physical wholeness but our spiritual well-being. After Jesus' declaration of forgiveness, the scribes immediately debate the authority of forgiving sins. Yet, as a disabled person, I notice what doesn't happen. When the man's sins are declared forgiven, he does not get immediately healed. If sin is so clearly linked to disability, you would expect him to be healed as soon as Jesus forgave his sins. By separating out forgiveness from healing, Jesus clearly, deliberately, delineates between sin and sickness. The delayed healing is not principally for the education of the crowd but a pastoral restoration for the suffering and excluded disabled man.

2 A sabbath for all

Mark 2:23—3:6

Disabled people successfully lobbied for the Americans with Disabilities Act (ADA) which passed in 1990, obliging public buildings and transport to include access for wheelchair users. However, one group successfully campaigned for an exemption so that they wouldn't have to comply: the church. Thousands of Christians objected to the law, partly because they wanted to be able to discriminate against people with AIDS. The exemption holds today for churches and Christian schools. If we're searching for today's equivalents to the religious leaders in Mark 3 who chose tradition over compassion for disabled people, we need not look too far.

The Pharisees objected to Jesus 'disrespecting' God's sabbath by 'doing work' on the holy day, first by Jesus plucking grain. Jesus argued through David's precedent in 1 Samuel 21 that the intention of the sabbath is blessing, 'The sabbath was made for humankind, and not humankind for the sabbath, so the Son of Man is lord even of the sabbath' (2:27–28).

When a man with a 'withered hand' (3:1), possibly as a result of cerebral palsy or a stroke, was in the synagogue with Jesus on the sabbath, the stakes were raised further. The Jewish guidance for applying the Mosaic law was that healing was not considered 'work' if it were a situation of life and death. However, if it were a non-emergency, the healing should wait until after the sabbath.

Jesus challenges their interpretation of the law by setting out stark choices: 'Is it lawful to do good or do harm on the sabbath, to save life or to kill?' (3:4). He is referencing Moses' great sermon in Deuteronomy, 'See, I set before you today life and prosperity, death and destruction… Now choose life' (Deuteronomy 30:15, 19). Ultimately, the Pharisees choose Jesus' death (3:6).

Only Mark's telling of this pericope identifies Jesus' angry and grief-filled response to the Pharisees' cold silence (v. 5). The man does not have to prove his worthiness for healing or display any sort of faith; Jesus simply heals him without ceremony, almost passively (v. 5). Healing people who needed it was not merely about showing Jesus' authority or correcting theological views, it is always, above all, an act of kindness for a dearly loved individual. Religion must never override compassion.

3 Women, stigma and silence

Mark 5:21–34

The woman crumples in despair as the doctor dismisses her bleeding as 'heavy periods' and laughs at his own joke about Eve bringing feminine pain into the world. Ashamed, she seeks private medics whose treatments are extortionate and harmful. The loss of blood renders her permanently iron-deficient and exhausted; her health deteriorates and her bank balance empties. This is as true for many women today as it was for the woman Jesus met.

For her, however, it also carried a religious stigma. Josephus confirmed that even in Jesus' time women were not allowed in the temple if they had menstrual bleeding (*B.J.*, 5.227), and she could not go near a Jewish man without making him unclean, ruling out children and marriage. What does it do to your psyche to constantly be shunned and shamed because of your female body?

Jairus is named, respected and has a voice (vv. 21–24). He is deemed worthy of Jesus' help. The anonymous woman, like the paralysed man of Mark 2, must break something to reach Jesus: in this case, the Jewish law. The method of healing is unique, without petition or an advocate; her prayer is silent and superstitious, simply touching his clothes, hoping to steal a healing. It is entirely the wrong approach and theology, but there is no other option for her. It shouldn't work: Jesus is not a magic totem and none of the crowd pressing in are cured. As Jesus apparently did not intend to heal her (vv. 28–30), maybe this is an instance where God the Father healed someone through Jesus.

Perhaps because of her experience of social rejection, the woman approaches Jesus with what Martin Buber calls an 'I:It' relationship, treating him as an object for her own goals. Jesus responds with an 'I:Thou' approach. Although she is already healed, Jesus seeks relationship. It is the only time Jesus calls someone 'daughter' (*thugater*, v. 34). He affirms her, 'Your faith has made you well'; confirms her healing is permanent and blesses her (v. 34). The biggest blessing is potentially Jesus validating her suffering, using the word *mastigos*, from *mastix*, whip. Her illness was like being flayed, and Jesus saw that. Even when healing does not come, women whose pain is dismissed still benefit from Jesus calling them daughter and the acknowledgement that their condition is daily torment.

4 Deafness and compassion

Mark 7:31-37

First, we must note it is extremely offensive to many Deaf people to suggest they need healing at all, and we should never presume that a Deaf (or indeed any disabled) person wants a cure. It's more common for those who lose their hearing in later life to view deafness as something to be corrected. People who are Deaf from early childhood use sign language as their first language and are embraced in Deaf culture and community, using interpreters as necessary for interactions with the hearing world. Being Deaf is a precious identity and they do not require hearing to live life well. Deafness is not a deficiency, merely a difference.

However, in Jesus' time the deaf man was likely to be significantly disabled by society. The word *kōphon* can mean either 'deaf' or 'deaf and speechless' so, to avoid doubt, Mark adds *mogilálon*, with *mógis* meaning 'hardly', or 'with difficulty' and *laliá* meaning 'speech' (v. 32). This recalls Isaiah, 'Then the... ears of the deaf [shall be] unstopped... and the tongue of the speechless [*mogilálōn*] sing for joy' (Isaiah 35:5-6). The regions of Tyre and Sidon (v. 31) are the same region as Isaiah's Lebanon (Isaiah 35:2). Mark is communicating that the eschatological Day of the Lord has arrived through Jesus.

Theologians puzzle over the unusual method by which Jesus heals the man. Rather than simply '[laying] his hand on him' as was expected (v. 32), Jesus instead 'took him aside in private... and put his fingers into his ears, and he spat and touched his tongue' (v. 33), only speaking a prayer to heaven once this was done (v. 34). Commentators suggest that the privacy element might be part of Mark's messianic secret (v. 36), and that spittle was often used as a healing treatment.

However, what I observe is a healer sensitive to the needs of a Deaf person about to hear for the first time. The noise of the crowd would have been overwhelming and cacophonous, so Jesus took him 'away from the crowd' (v. 33). Since the man can't hear speech, Jesus compassionately explains through touch what he is about to do, hence his fingers in his ears and on his tongue before the healing comes. Jesus is never formulaic but creatively responds to each individual's needs.

5 Disability and demons

Mark 9:14–29; Matthew 17:15

Jesus was asked to help a boy. The details of his affliction are thus: he is unable to hear or speak (Mark 9:17, 25); on occasion, he falls dramatically, sometimes dangerously into 'the fire and into the water' (v. 22), and 'he foams and grinds his teeth and becomes rigid' (v. 18). When Jesus saw him, immediately the boy experienced convulsions (v. 20). What is the diagnosis?

In Mark's account, the father attributed it to a 'spirit' (*pneuma*) (vv. 17–21). Matthew's truncated version hints at an Ancient Greek folk explanation through the word *selēniazetai*, which literally means someone who is 'moonstruck' (Matthew 17:15), from which came our English word 'lunatic'. Some believed it was punishment by the moon goddess Selene. Aristotle attributed periodic medical conditions with the moon's pull. Even today, up to 81% of mental health professionals believe that mental illness worsens during a full moon, despite several studies disproving this theory statistically. Modern readers tend to be nervous of demons, asserting the boy's condition is severe mental illness, autism or, most commonly, epilepsy. Indeed, the NRSV editors have taken the liberty of translating 'moonstruck' in Matthew 17:15 as 'epileptic', presumably based on the description in Mark 9. It is more accurate to say they diagnosed him rather than translated the Greek.

However, Jesus doesn't heal a disease but casts out a demon: '[Jesus] rebuked the unclean spirit, saying… "I command you, come out of him"' (v. 25). As Roy McCloughry, a writer with epilepsy, points out in his book *The Enabled Life*, this leaves us with a puzzle. There are four explanations: 1) this was not an illness but demon possession, and the NRSV needs to be retranslated (my choice), 2) Jesus didn't know it was epilepsy because he was limited in his knowledge and thought it was a demon (and this exorcism supposedly cured a boy of epilepsy), 3) Jesus knew it was epilepsy but pretended it was demonic, or 4) it was epilepsy and epilepsy is caused by demons.

This is not a theoretical issue. Sangeeta Persaud, a Guyanese teenager, died in 2010 because pastors pounded on her body to 'exorcise' her seizure, and Torrance Cantrell, an American eight-year-old autistic boy, died in 2003 while being restrained by church leaders to 'exorcise' his autism. It is abusive and potentially fatal to mislabel illness or neurodivergence as demonic.

6 Disability and begging

Mark 10:46–52

It is costly to be disabled. Assuming a disabled person is already receiving the disability benefit of DLA/PIP, which helps a little to level the playing field, disability charity Scope calculates that disabled people in the UK in 2023 still incur extra costs of £1,122 per month (more than £12k per year) to maintain the same basic standard of living as non-disabled people. Those who have applied for disability benefits know that it is a complicated system designed to deny disabled people the money they're entitled to and will humiliate you in the process. The government estimates fraud levels of DLA/PIP at just 0.2%, but the myth persists that disability payments are easy to get and fraud is rife. Make no mistake, however sophisticated the process may look, disabled people still have to beg today in order to make ends meet.

Bartimaeus is introduced as 'a blind man' (identified by his disability), who sits 'by the roadside' (peripheral to society, literally marginalised), 'begging' (Mark 10:46, NIV). I am curious, therefore, as to why Bartimaeus wants to be healed. Was it because he wanted to see, in and of itself, or was it because he was sick of living a precarious existence that depended on the whim of others, having to present himself as somehow worthy of pity, worthy of charity? It can be tempting to read Jesus' healing ministry purely as a physiological issue, but this passage reminds us how social justice and disability are intertwined.

Today, we subconsciously expect disabled people to be humble and grateful for any handouts or kindness they receive and to be passive recipients: heads down, voices soft in supplication. Bartimaeus wonderfully defies these expectations. While 'many sternly ordered him to be quiet' (v. 48), he cries out, creatively using the power of his voice to overcome the limitations of his sight. Bartimaeus insists he has as much right to receive from Jesus as anyone else. This is often what faith looks like: reasonable requests, boldly given. For his unapologetic faith, he is healed (v. 52). By the end of the story, he is no longer 'by the roadside' (v. 46, NIV) but literally 'on the road' (v. 52, my own translation). With his newfound independence, he chooses to follow Jesus. This passage invites us to see disabled people as determined disciples, not disgraced beggars.

Guidelines

- What most shocks you about the struggles disabled people face in society and the church today?
- Think of your local church and do an imaginary disability audit of how welcoming the services are for:
  - wheelchair users
  - neurodivergent people (autistic people, those with ADHD, those with sensory sensitivities, dyslexic people and those with Tourette's syndrome, etc.)
  - Deaf people and those who are hard of hearing
  - blind and partially sighted people
  - people with anxiety or depression and other mental illnesses
  - people with dementia
  - people who need quick access to a toilet
  - people who are housebound
- What do you notice so far about how Jesus interacts with disabled people? What do you think 'healing' might look like today, and is it necessarily the same as 'cure'?
- Regarding the study on the word 'moonstruck', how would you choose to translate that word in the Bible text? Which interpretation would you choose of the boy's condition, and why?
- To what extent does our society link sin with sickness? To what extent do you believe this for yourself, either consciously or subconsciously?
- One theme of Jesus' encounters with disabled people is compassion and anger at injustice. If you are disabled or chronically ill, what might it look like for you to fully receive Jesus' compassion? What does it mean to you that Jesus is angry with injustice?

25–31 August

1 Sickness as punishment

Luke 5:12–16; Leviticus 13:40–46

A man with a skin disease comes to Jesus. It's unlikely to be Hansen's disease, what we today call 'leprosy', and it is not necessarily highly contagious. From the description of the Hebrew word ṣāra'aṭ in Leviticus 13, it could encompass vitiligo, impetigo, various types of dermatitis, psoriasis, etc.

In Moses' day, this illness meant spiritual and social isolation; 'he shall live alone', outside the camp (Leviticus 13:46) and was forbidden from the tabernacle. It was humiliating, too: you had to announce your presence to others with torn clothing and dishevelled hair, crying, 'unclean, unclean' (v. 45).

Elsewhere in the Hebrew Bible, ṣāra'aṭ is associated with God's punishment for sin: God strikes Miriam with ṣāra'aṭ for defying Moses (Numbers 12:10) and King Uzziah for offering incense (2 Chronicles 26:16-21). Though scholars differ on the degree of social isolation people with these conditions experienced in Jesus' day, they were at least excluded from temple worship and were likely still associated with God's judgement. To have 'leprosy' in Jesus' day was to be viewed as the personification of God's judgement on sin.

No wonder the man 'bowed with his face to the ground and begged [Jesus]' (Luke 5:12), such was his shame and desperation. His request, 'make me clean' (v. 12), shows his most pressing need was not healing from physical discomfort but the end of isolation from worship and society. Is Jesus endorsing the cruel discrimination against chronically sick people by insisting on adhering to Moses' laws (v. 14)? Only Luke's version of the healing offers an interpretation of why the man must see the priests, 'for a testimony for them' (v. 14), rather than needing purification himself. Jesus is operating outside the temple system, potentially defying it.

What diseases today do we subconsciously view as judgement for sin, though we logically know the medical cause? Though AIDS is decreasing in stigma, some Christians regrettably still view it as God's punishment of gay people. Other diseases are assumed to be caused by promiscuity. Many Christians interpret alcoholism as a moral failing, though it has a large genetic and physiological component. Depression is suspected to be a lack of Christian joy, anxiety as a lack of trust in God. Do people with these conditions feel safe to worship in our church? That's the challenge from the passage today.

2 Faith healing

Luke 7:1–10

I've been to various Pentecostal and evangelical healing services where the expectation is that you must first confess all your sins, then believe without wavering that you will be healed, then pray for healing, and finally declare that you have been healed, even if nothing feels different, thus demonstrating your faith. God's healing is seen as a guaranteed transactional exchange, and the strength of the cure depends on the strength of the faith.

Though this passage involves faith and Jesus' healing, it is quite different from our current society's understanding of 'faith healing'. It is worth noting that the slave, who was 'close to death' (v. 2), was not required to have faith for his own healing. Indeed, he may not have been conscious. It is a heavy burden that some parts of the church put on physically depleted and emotionally exhausted people to somehow contribute to their healing by conjuring an impossible level of faith and holiness.

Matthew has an abbreviated version of this story in which the centurion himself appeals to Jesus in person. In Luke, the centurion's point about his ability to command others is proven in that he never even meets Jesus. We have the combined faith of the 'Jewish elders' (v. 3), who petition Jesus to come back to the centurion's house, then his 'friends' (*philous*) (v. 6), who deliver the centurion's message verbatim in first-person narrative. It is fascinating that although Jesus could heal without being anywhere near the sick person, he was initially happy to do what was expected and travel to the house. Why was this? Perhaps it was for reasons of compassion, or because Jesus was working within their expectations.

We also see that Jesus' miraculous healings, when they occur, are not limited to those within the faith community. Though the Jews report the centurion 'loves our people' and built a synagogue (v. 5), there's no indication that he was a proselyte. Here, an anonymous slave is healed by a foreigner's faith without Jesus even being nearby. Jesus marvelled in the centurion's trust in and understanding of his authority (v. 9). To have faith like the centurion is to understand that we do not engineer our healing by our faith or good deeds, we merely petition the one with power. The centurion does not know that Jesus *will* heal, only that he can.

3 Chronic illness and condemnation

John 5:1–16

The list of commentators queuing up to vilify the chronically ill man healed by Jesus is shockingly long. Jesus' question, 'Do you want to be made well?' (John 5:6) is seen as a test of faith, which the man fails by omitting a definite 'yes'. The fact that he doesn't have a friend to help him into the water is dismissed as a weak excuse: clearly, he doesn't want to be healed. One theologian quoted a racist proverb of people preferring begging to healing. Jesus' words, 'Do not sin any more' (v. 14), are interpreted as his sin having caused his sickness, and 'so that nothing worse happens to you' (v. 14) is Jesus threatening to withdraw the healing if he continues sinning. Finally, he is seen as especially stupid or evil for initially not knowing who healed him (v. 13), and then for later naming Jesus as his healer (v. 15) because this led to 'the Jews... persecuting Jesus' (v. 16).

I am that lame man, and I feel those stings personally. He had been living in desperate limbo for 38 years; for me, it's been almost 15 years of being mainly bedbound. Society is very sympathetic to acute suffering but less sympathetic as the suffering continues. Eventually, people are blamed for their misfortune. If I reject an alternative medicine suggestion, often the suggester becomes hostile and claims I want to remain ill. My sickness has also been blamed on my sin and my personality.

The man, with no hope of medical cure, is desperate for alternative medicine, but his disability prevents him from accessing the 'magic' cure of the disturbed waters. When Jesus asks if he wants to be well, it is not a test but a compassionate offer of help. Though the man can't see beyond the pool as the mechanism of his healing, Jesus swiftly heals him with a command, with no appeal to confession or declaration of forgiveness. Jesus' words about sinning in verse 14 should be read in the context of John 9:1–2, where Jesus resists associating sickness with sin, and Luke 13, where Jesus explains that the victims of the Tower of Siloam falling were not worse sinners, but 'unless you repent, you will all perish' (Luke 13:5). The 'something worse' of Jesus' warning to the man is therefore eschatological and a warning for us all.

4 Disability and personhood

John 9:1–34

When is a blind man not a blind man? When he is a theological problem instead. The disciples are certain that disability is caused by sin, but for someone born blind, how could they have already sinned? Was it the parents' sin (v. 2)? Jesus repudiates the idea that either party's sin caused the blindness, which is surely a comfort, but continues, 'He was born blind so that God's works might be revealed in him' (v. 3). Does this then mean that his blindness was given so that he might be healed by Jesus one day? How is that fair? It is worth pointing out that there is no punctuation in the ancient texts, and the phrase 'he was born blind' has been inserted into the NRSV; it is simply not there in the Greek. Though few commentators choose this option, it's very possible (and preferable?) that it should be translated, 'Neither this man nor his parents sinned. So that God's works might be revealed in him, we must work the works of him who sent me...' (vv. 3–4).

Once healed, the man becomes a theological problem for the neighbours and Pharisees. The crowd understood healing from congenital blindness to be impossible. Surely, then, it was a different man (v. 9). For the Pharisees, the problem is Jesus healing him. If a healing is to be done, it is by God, so God should get the glory ('Give glory to God!' v. 24), and God would never heal on the sabbath (v. 16). Therefore, either he is not healed, he was not born blind or Jesus healed him demonically. Either way, Jesus is a sinner (v. 24). The Pharisees' final rejection of the man is illuminating and shocking, 'You were born entirely in sins' (v. 34). Even when the man is no longer blind, they retain their ableist label of him as a sinner, inferior to them.

In response to the neighbours' confusion over identity, the healed man answers simply, 'I am' (v. 9): the words 'that man' are not there in the Greek text. Still today, strangers often only see impairment, inferiority or sinfulness in disabled people, and disabled people have to remind others that they are not a theological problem to be solved but a person who is.

25–31 August

5 Disability as metaphor

John 9:24–41

'What, are you blind?' someone might say to a friend who is refusing to agree with their point. They don't mean blind, of course, they mean wilfully ignorant. If leaders are ill-equipped for a task, we might say, 'It's the blind leading the blind', words lifted from Jesus' condemnation of the Pharisees (Matthew 15:14). I think of my blind friend, Lyndall Bywater, who happily leads other blind friends along any route familiar to her. When she was younger, she would even lead her other friends back from the pub in one long crocodile, as she was simply blind, and they were, as she put it, 'blind drunk' and needed her help. The pejorative phrases that use blindness as a metaphor for lostness, sin or ignorance ironically contradict the reality of being blind.

Jesus' encounter with the formerly blind man concludes with revelation and metaphor. We have witnessed his growing understanding of Jesus' identity, initially describing him as 'the man called Jesus' (v. 11), then 'a prophet' (v. 17), 'one who worships [God] and obeys his will' (v. 31), and 'from God' (v. 33). At the point where the religious community have excommunicated him and proclaimed him morally inferior, Jesus seeks him out to encourage and teach him (v. 35). Meeting Jesus again, the man eagerly accepts Jesus' self-identification as the 'Son of Man' figure, the king with all authority whom the prophet Daniel saw in a vision from God (Daniel 7:13–14). Climactically, 'he worshipped him' (v. 38), pledging his allegiance and obedience to Jesus.

Summarising his own mission, Jesus contrasts the physical healing of the blind man with the spiritual obstinacy of the Pharisees, 'I came into this world for judgement so that those who do not see may see' (literally) 'and those who do see may become blind' (metaphorically) (v. 39).

Notwithstanding Jesus' use of blindness as metaphor, it is overall a liberatory passage for blind people, focusing as it does on the man's quick wit and growing faith rather than purely a display of Jesus' power. The formerly blind man now has sight, but more importantly demonstrates great insight, and he is an exemplary disciple. Jesus challenges any potential smugness of sighted people as he values spiritual understanding more highly than literal vision.

6 Celebrating disabled bodies

John 20:19–29

I once asked a sample of disabled people, 'Supposing you had the choice: would you want to keep your disability in heaven?' A significant minority of disabled people said yes. It was so much a treasured part of their identity that they couldn't conceive of being 'them' without it.

Until Jesus' resurrection appearances, so many people are healed of their disability and illness that we could be forgiven for thinking that there was only room in God's kingdom for people with bodies corrected and 'perfected' to able-bodied norms. Was there even a place for a disabled follower of Jesus? Yet here we have Jesus in his resurrected body, displaying either wounds or scars from his crucifixion (v. 20, 25, 27). Nancy Eiesland, in her notable book *The Disabled God*, points to Jesus' resurrection body as symbolic of a God with disability, describing his hands, feet and side as 'impaired'. In much of Christian understanding, she explains, we have a model of Christ as either 'suffering servant' or 'conquering lord'. This echoes society's picture of disability – if you do not have an abled body, then you are a sufferer, a victim, unless perhaps you are a Paralympian who has overcome their disability. Jesus' resurrected body presents a different, more positive picture of disability, that of 'survivor'.

Others have objected to the language of disability or impairment in Christ's resurrected body. After all, his body is less limited than before: he can be miraculously present in a room despite locked doors (vv. 19, 26). At the very least, however, we can state that Jesus' body is disfigured. Jesus' invitation for Thomas to put his hand in his side raises the intriguing possibility of whether there was an opening still there and whether it was a wound that was miraculously free from infection, or a scar that nevertheless left some kind of gap. The Greeks would eschew the physical entirely, and the Jews would want perfection in the body, but Jesus shows off his blemished, sinless body without shame.

In these twelve studies, we have seen that although abled people locate the problem of disability in the body, the social and spiritual stigmas of disability are the real issue. While Jesus does not cure everyone who wants it today, disabled people still encounter shame, rejection, poverty, loneliness, exclusion from worship spaces and literal demonisation, and there is much that Christ's body, the church, can do to heal this.

Guidelines

- Which conditions or illnesses are particularly stigmatised by society or the church today? Which conditions or illnesses do you naturally feel less comfortable about? What are the reasons behind this?
- What do you understand by 'faith healing'? How comfortable do you feel in praying for others' or your own healing, and when might you want to avoid that prayer? How can the church sensitively offer healing prayer?
- Try a language audit to practise awareness of how it might sound to disabled people – list all the phrases that use disability and metaphor and 'translate' them into what we actually mean by them without using disability language. For example, 'blind spot', 'tone deaf', 'turn a blind eye to', 'maniac', 'a bit OCD', 'crippling poverty', 'lame excuse', 'they're mental', 'that's crazy', 'falling on deaf ears', 'I was blind but now I see', 'suicide mission', words like 'moron, imbecile, idiot'.
- Most people are good at compassion for acute suffering but less good with ongoing suffering. To what extent have you seen this in yourself? Who do you know who has capacity for ongoing compassion and empathy?
- Nancy Eiesland's three categories for the messiah were 'suffering servant', 'conquering lord' and 'survivor'. How do these labels help you meditate on the person of Christ? To what extent do you associate these labels with disabled people? What label best fits you?
- How has this series changed your reading of the healing miracles? What will you take away from this?

FURTHER READING

Martin Buber, *I and Thou* (Howard Books, 2008).
Nancy Eiesland, *The Disabled God* (Abingdon Press, 1994).
John Hull, *In the Beginning There was Darkness* (SCM Press, 2001).
Roy McCloughry, *The Enabled Life: Christianity in a disabling world* (SPCK, 2013).
Sarah Melcher, Mikeal Parsons and Amos Yong (eds), *The Bible and Disability: A commentary* (Baylor University Press, 2017).
Candida Moss and Jeremy Schipper (eds), *Disability Studies and Biblical Literature* (Palgrave Macmillan, 2011).
John Pilch, *Healing in the New Testament: Insights from medical and Mediterranean anthropology* (Fortress Press, 2000).

SHARING OUR VISION – MAKING A GIFT

I would like to make a donation to support BRF Ministries.
Please use my gift for:

- [ ] Where it is most needed
- [ ] Anna Chaplaincy
- [ ] Living Faith
- [ ] Messy Church
- [ ] Parenting for Faith

Title	First name/initials	Surname

Address

	Postcode

Email

Telephone

Signature	Date

Please accept my gift of:

- [ ] £2
- [ ] £5
- [ ] £10
- [ ] £20
- Other £ ☐

by (*delete as appropriate*):

- [ ] Cheque/Charity Voucher payable to 'BRF'
- [ ] MasterCard/Visa/Debit card/Charity card

Name on card

Card no. ☐☐☐☐ ☐☐☐☐ ☐☐☐☐ ☐☐☐☐

Expires end M M / Y Y Security code* ☐☐☐ *Last 3 digits on the reverse of the card

Signature	Date

Please complete other side of form

GL0125

SHARING OUR VISION – MAKING A GIFT

BRF Ministries Gift Aid Declaration
In order to Gift Aid your donation, you must tick the box below.

☐ I want to Gift Aid my donation and any donation I make in the future or have made in the past four years to BRF Ministries

I am a UK taxpayer and understand that if I pay less Income Tax and/or Capital Gains Tax in the current tax year than the amount of Gift Aid claimed on all my donations, it is my responsibility to pay any difference.

Please notify BRF Ministries if you want to cancel this Gift Aid declaration, change your name or home address, or no longer pay sufficient tax on your income and/or capital gains.

You can also give online at **brf.org.uk/donate**, which reduces our administration costs, making your donation go further.

Our ministry is only possible because of the generous support of individuals, churches, trusts and gifts in wills.

☐ I would like to leave a gift to BRF Ministries in my will.
   Please send me further information.

☐ I would like to find out about giving a regular gift to BRF Ministries.

For help or advice regarding making a gift, please contact our fundraising team +44 (0)1235 462305

Your privacy

We will use your personal data to process this transaction. From time to time we may send you information about the work of BRF Ministries that we think may be of interest to you. Our privacy policy is available at **brf.org.uk/privacy**. Please contact us if you wish to discuss your mailing preferences.

Registered with

FR

FUNDRAISING **REGULATOR**

● Please complete other side of form

Please return this form to 'Freepost BRF'
No other address information or stamp is needed

Bible Reading Fellowship is a charity (233280) and company limited by guarantee (301324), registered in England and Wales

GL0125

Overleaf… Guidelines forthcoming issue | Author profile | Recommended reading | Order and subscription forms

Guidelines forthcoming issue

The coming September issue of *Guidelines* is full of very good things! In the run-up to Advent and Christmas, it's important to take the time to prepare your heart and mind for the season; hopefully the next issue will be a helpful companion.

In the New Testament, Ashley Hibbard tackles 1 Chronicles which, like Numbers, can be considered dry and difficult. Ashley shows us how these books (she will also write on 2 Chronicles in the January issue) showcase a people at a volatile turning point in their history, able only to cling to the goodness of God. Perhaps we can relate in our own times. Joel Barker reflects on Zechariah, which also addresses God's people post-exile. Meanwhile Amy Scott Robinson, a poet and storyteller, looks at the Psalms through the lens of seeing them as poetry; how can understanding the conventions of Hebrew poetry enlighten our readings of the Psalms and turn them to prayer?

Our deep dive into Acts continues with Isabelle Hamley, who takes us through this period of church growth as well as struggles. Ian Paul gives us a whisle-stop tour through the short books of 1, 2 and 3 John, while Sharon Prentis focuses in on the parables of Jesus in the book of Matthew.

Nick Page, who works for Open Doors, has provided two weeks of study on persecution, focusing on the New Testament experience of persecution and what parallels we can draw to the persecuted church in modern times. He also invites us to think about what this means for how we express our faith in our culture, and, ultimately, how we respond to the persecution and suffering of our worldwide family.

As we move into Advent, we spend two weeks with Max Kramer as he reflects on signs of Jesus' coming. Using both familiar and less familiar Advent readings, he invites us to read these passages in their full context instead of cherry-picking particular verses, as often happens.

Finally, we have two fascinating sets of thematic notes. Charmaine Mhlanga reflects on AI (artificial intelligence) and asks rather than answers plenty of questions about this up-and-coming technology and how we might respond to it. Andy Angel, meanwhile, explores the common biblical myth of God as a divine warrior figure, and how the biblical authors used this image to speak the living word of God into the lives of the covenant people.

What the Bible means to me: Tanya Marlow

When I was a child, the Bible was a magical book. It had fairy-tale elements: God created the world out of nothing, like Cinderella's fairy-godmother made coaches from pumpkins and footmen from frogs; Jack killed the giant using a beanstalk, like David slew a giant with a sling; Rumpelstiltskin prophesied the birth of a child like a twisted version of the Old Testament prophets. Even from a young age, however, I knew there was a big difference. A fairytale was magic because it was not true, whereas the Bible was magic because it was true.

Reciting a favourite passage from my most beloved childhood novels was enjoyable, but nothing compared to the power of reading out a beloved Bible verse and knowing it was written just for me. As a teenager, when stuck for inspiration or guidance, I played Bible lottery, where you close your eyes, open the Bible at random, and then whatever your finger lands on would be God's message to you. Sometimes, it was just a bunch of genealogies, but other times, the passage was eerily applicable to my life.

Then in my late teens and twenties I studied the Bible academically, and it took away some of the technicolour dream quality of my beloved stories. It was no longer a love letter from God to me, full of incantation and mystery, but a book of architecture, dust and history. I had thought of the words as permanently set in stone, echoing from generation to generation, but now there were translation variations and debates about meaning. Scholars sought to squash the miraculous out of the text and make it grey and lifeless so it could be easily contained, rational and explainable. The Bible almost crumbled and crashed before my eyes, but I began to see it as a deeper, perhaps darker, more complex story of humanity's relationship with God, with fewer clear heroes and villains.

When I became disabled with a debilitating illness, I needed the Bible to be more than a happy story or a set of spells to make life better; I needed complexity and nuance. I looked to Job for ranting and lament, to John the Baptist for a life lived without resolution, and to Naomi for her honest bitterness.

But the point I want to make is not that I started off with a naive understanding of God's word and ended up becoming more mature. It is rather that God meets us wherever we are in the pages of the Bible and can speak to us through it in multiple ways.

The Bible is still a magical book. The Spirit of God leaps from the words to my heart, sometimes cutting me to the quick, sometimes placing balm on my soul. Whenever I read it with prayer, something fresh appears, whether that's an intellectual insight or a wordless shift in my inner being, and I am transformed from one thing to another. If that's not magic, I don't know what is.

Recommended reading

Is this all there is to faith? Every Christian carries a map, a mental image of their journey through life, created from their Christian tradition, their cultural background and their understanding of the Bible. Many Christians will also, at some point in their life, begin to question their map – causing them to ask, 'Is this all there is?' and 'How did I get here?'

In *Reimagining the Landscape of Faith*, Mary and Charles Hippsley help us to identify our faith map, including the unexamined assumptions that underpin it. Then, drawing on a range of sources of wisdom, including personal experience, they gently encourage us to allow God to expand our map when we find that our faith doesn't match up with the reality of life. They aim to equip the reader to navigate their journey towards maturity by exploring new paths and landscapes of faith.

Reimagining the Landscape of Faith
Essential pathways for spiritual growth

The following is an edited extract taken from chapter 4, 'Where are you on your journey?'.

When attempting to navigate through the Lakeland Fells or the peat bogs of Dartmoor the determined traveller needs the most detailed Ordnance Survey maps available, known as the Explorer Series. At a scale of 4 cm to 1 km, it takes 403 Explorer maps to cover Great Britain, and that means you'll probably need several maps for a walking holiday in a big national park. Typically, as I unpacked my rucksack to tackle one of these kinds of treks, I would discover that I'd brought three of the four I needed for that trip but had left the crucial one at home!

On our spiritual journey, it's natural for us to stick to the first map we are given. But relying on that one map to see us through our entire Christian journey has its limitations. We learn lots of helpful things about our faith and the God we worship. We learn to pray in certain ways, and it shows us how to serve our church community and perhaps the wider community as well. But after a while many disciples, me included, may recognise that nothing much substantial has changed inside us. I do sense and enjoy God's presence with me, but I'm still the same old me. Even though I may have recognised my 'spiritual gifts' (Romans 12), the same temptations trip me up (Romans 7) and consistently manifesting fruits of the Spirit that truly reflect godly character

(Galatians 5) is sadly lacking. It's like I've changed my function and appearance on the outside, but not the reality of myself on the inside.

But that twinge of discontent we feel when we recognise how far we have still to go is not a bad thing. It's like God is touching our hearts with his love and encouraging us to draw closer, go deeper, unquestionably become more like Christ as well as doing our best to act like him. So, what is it that can hinder that deeper transformation we are promised as new creations in Christ (2 Corinthians 5:17)?

Perhaps that initial map we hold just doesn't cover enough ground to get us there. And as we explored in chapter 2, we'd benefit from examining it again and updating it. Drawn as it is with selection and emphasis influenced by certain cultural and Christian assumptions our map may be incomplete or missing some critical dimensions or regions. And we can expand our horizons, allowing ourselves to be enriched by the writings of other Christians who have walked this way before us – including perhaps some whose perspective is beyond our own tradition.

However, wherever we are on our map, once we feel that call onward it is imperative that we don't just 'stay there', assuming that whatever we are perceiving or experiencing today represents all there is or will be on the path of discipleship!

Every time explorers set out to discover new territories and extended the boundaries of their cultural spheres, cartographical evidence had to be drawn quickly to lay claim to those discoveries. In the early years of exploring the Americas, for example, Sebastian Münster published a map in 1540 that showed the Spanish flag over the West Indies. The problem was, his focus on this valuable region left the rest of North America somewhat underrepresented! This must have been very confusing for subsequent explorers, who expected to see a thin strip of land only to find out as they pushed further west how vast the New World actually was.

I wonder if we're a bit like that. How much do we know or want to know about ourselves? Are we curious enough to keep pushing beyond the territory that we've already discovered and lies within our current consciousness?

To this end, I've noticed something odd about our stories of faith. Where we begin that story makes a big difference! If our story begins in Genesis 3 rather than Genesis 1, then faith tends to be grounded in the fall of humanity and the shame of our sin rather than in the glory of our humanity being made to carry the very image of God. The first perspective offers us an image focused on worthlessness and corruption and draws us to the work of Jesus on the cross in restoring our relationship with God – for which we are so grateful. But going back to include the creation stories in Genesis 1—2 also recognises that, while we are deeply flawed and need that restored relationship with God, the seed of God's original intent remains in our soul at the centre of our being, albeit covered by layers of self-inflicted shame.

It's not that one story cancels out the other; it's more a question of selection and emphasis. And that emphasis is crucial in determining our expectation for growing in the likeness of Christ.

When we came to Christ, we brought with us the mask we had constructed with which to face the world, with all of its robust defences and protective layers born out of the nature, nurture and trauma we had experienced up to that point. A lot of our perception of and relationship with God and those around us can be determined by that defended-self, together with the shame it carries. And yet it doesn't represent the fullness of who God created us to be, the nature of our soul and the image of God we carry, if you like. In order to grow to the place from which we have the freedom to operate out of that God-given fullness, we first need to become aware of the role our defended-self plays in day-to-day life.

To order a copy of Reimagining the Landscape of Faith, *use the order form on page 153 or visit* **brfonline.org.uk**

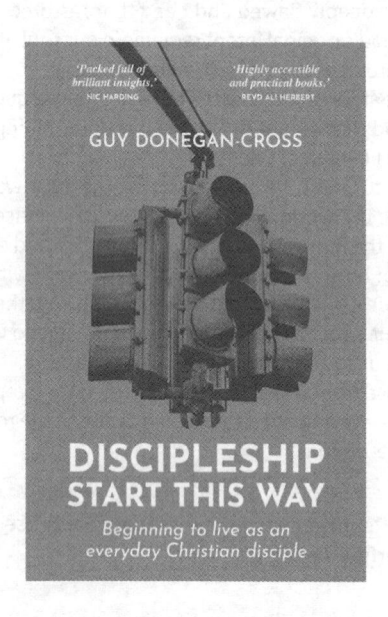

Discipleship: Start This Way is the first of two books which inform individuals or groups in being Christian disciples, with a distinctive emphasis on the difference discipleship makes in our everyday experience of life. It is both a resource for the person who wants to explore Christian discipleship and a tool for anyone wanting to support someone in beginning their faith journey.

Discipleship: Start This Way
Beginning to live as an everyday Christian disciple
Guy Donegan-Cross
978 1 80039 375 2 £9.99
brfonline.org.uk

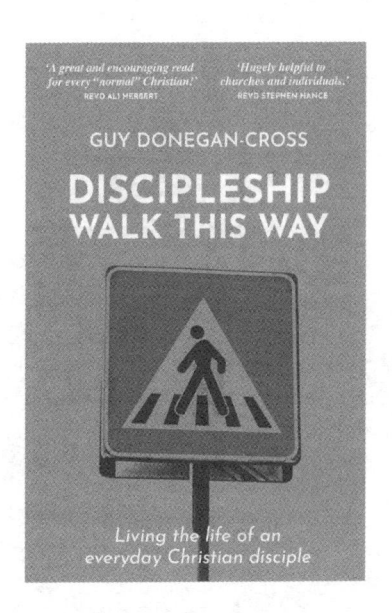

How does it feel to grow and live as an everyday Christian disciple? *Discipleship: Walk This Way* is the second of two books which inform individuals or groups in being Christian disciples. It is a resource for the new Christian who is asking, 'What now?' or the long-term Christian who is wondering, 'So what?' Through personal stories and accessible teaching it unpacks the lifestyle of being with God, the meaning of Christian character and how it grows, and the aim of a disciple in all of life.

Discipleship: Walk This Way
Living the life of an everyday Christian disciple
Guy Donegan-Cross
978 1 80039 373 8 £14.99
brfonline.org.uk

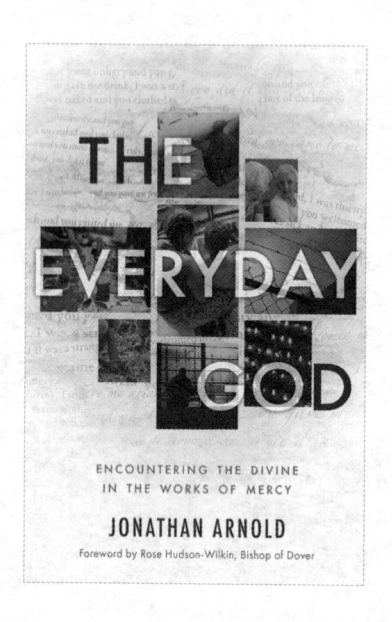

Jonathan Arnold, a seasoned community engagement expert, delves deep into the heart of the biblical mandate to love one's neighbour. Through a tapestry of real-life stories, he unveils the power of practical faith, illustrating how it can ignite transformation among the poor and vulnerable. As he reflects upon Jesus' teaching in Matthew 25:34–40, Arnold challenges us to discover God's presence in the most unexpected places and join in with where he is acting, whether inside or outside our churches.

The Everyday God
Encountering the Divine in the works of mercy
Jonathan Arnold
978 1 80039 210 6 £9.99
brfonline.org.uk

Through revelations ten to sixteen of her *Revelations of Divine Love*, Julian of Norwich returns time and again to the idea that 'all is well', and Emma Pennington examines this popular mantra and explores what Julian really means by it, bringing depth and relevance to these words for the reader who lives in an age of pandemic, war and climate crisis which closely echoes Julian's own. Deep engagement with Julian's visions of salvation encourages the reader to reflect in prayer and devotion on their own personal relationship with God.

All Shall Be Well
Visions of salvation with Julian of Norwich
Emma Pennington
978 1 80039 206 9 £12.99
brfonline.org.uk

Rhythms of Grace

Finding intimacy with God in a busy life

Tony Horsfall

In this fully revised and updated second edition of a classic book, Tony Horsfall shows how contemplative spirituality, with its emphasis on realising our identity as God's beloved children and on being rather than doing, has vital lessons for us about discovering intimacy with God. It also provides essential insights about building a ministry that is both enjoyable and sustainable.

Rhythms of Grace
Finding intimacy with God in a busy life
Tony Horsfall
978 1 80039 327 1 £9.99
brfonline.org.uk

To order

Online: brfonline.org.uk
Telephone: +44 (0)1865 319700
Mon–Fri 9.30–17.00

Delivery times within the UK are normally 15 working days. Prices are correct at the time of going to press but may change without prior notice.

BRF

Title	Price	Qty	Total
Reimagining the Landscape of Faith	£9.99		
Discipleship: Start This Way	£9.99		
Discipleship: Walk This Way	£14.99		
The Everyday God	£9.99		
All Shall Be Well	£12.99		
Rhythms of Grace new edition	£9.99		

POSTAGE AND PACKING CHARGES			
Order value	UK	Europe	Rest of world
Under £7.00	£2.00	Available on request	Available on request
£7.00–£29.99	£3.00		
£30.00 and over	FREE		

Total value of books	
Donation*	
Postage and packing	
Total for this order	

Please complete in BLOCK CAPITALS

*Please complete and return the Gift Aid declaration on page 140.

Title _____ First name/initials _____ Surname _____

Address _____

_____ Postcode _____

Acc. No. _____ Telephone _____

Email _____

Method of payment

❏ Cheque (made payable to BRF) ❏ MasterCard / Visa

Card no. ☐☐☐☐ ☐☐☐☐ ☐☐☐☐ ☐☐☐☐

Expires end M M Y Y Security code* ☐☐☐ *Last 3 digits on the reverse of the card

We will use your personal data to process this order. From time to time we may send you information about the work of BRF Ministries. Please contact us if you wish to discuss your mailing preferences.
brf.org.uk/privacy

Registered with FUNDRAISING REGULATOR

Please return this form to:
BRF Ministries, 15 The Chambers, Vineyard, Abingdon OX14 3FE | enquiries@brf.org.uk
For terms and cancellation information, please visit brfonline.org.uk/terms.

Bible Reading Fellowship is a charity (233280) and company limited by guarantee (301324), registered in England and Wales

BRF Ministries needs you!

If you're one of our regular *Guidelines* readers, you will know all about the benefits and blessings of regular Bible study and the value of serious daily notes to guide, inform and challenge you.

Here are some recent comments from *Guidelines* readers:

> *'... very thoughtful and spiritually helpful. [These notes] are speaking to the church as it is today, and therefore to Christians like us who live in today's world.'*

> *'You have assembled an amazingly diverse group of people and their contributions are most certainly thoughtful.'*

If you have similarly positive things to say about *Guidelines*, would you be willing to share your experience with others? Could you ask for a brief slot during church notices or write a short piece for your church magazine or website? Do you belong to groups, formal or informal, academic or professional, where you could share your experience of using *Guidelines* and encourage others to try them?

It doesn't need to be complicated: just answering these three questions in what you say or write will get your message across:

- How do *Guidelines* Bible study notes help you grow in knowledge and faith?
- Where, when and how do you use them?
- What would you say to people who haven't yet tried them?

We can supply further information if you need it and would love to hear about it if you do give a talk or write an article.

For more information:

- Email **enquiries@brf.org.uk**
- Telephone BRF Ministries on +44 (0)1865 319700 Mon–Fri 9.30–17.00
- Write to us at BRF Ministries, 15 The Chambers, Vineyard, Abingdon OX14 3FE

Inspiring people of all ages to grow in Christian faith

At BRF Ministries, we long for people of all ages to grow in faith and understanding of the Bible. That's what all our work as a charity is about.

- Our **Living Faith** range of resources helps Christians go deeper in their understanding of scripture, in prayer and in their walk with God. Our conferences and events bring people together to share this journey, while our Holy Habits resources help whole congregations grow together as disciples of Jesus, living out and sharing their faith.

- We also want to make it easier for local churches to engage effectively in ministry and mission – by helping them bring new families into a growing relationship with God through **Messy Church** or by supporting churches as they nurture the spiritual life of older people through **Anna Chaplaincy**.

- Our **Parenting for Faith** team coaches parents and others to raise God-connected children and teens, and enables churches to fully support them.

Do you share our vision?

Though a significant proportion of BRF Ministries' funding is generated through our charitable activities, we are dependent on the generous support of individuals, churches and charitable trusts.

If you share our vision, would you help us to enable even more people of all ages to grow in faith? Your prayers and financial support are vital for the work that we do. You could:

- Support BRF Ministries with a regular donation;
- Support us with a one-off gift;
- Consider leaving a gift to BRF Ministries in your will (see page 156);
- Encourage your church to support BRF Ministries as part of your church's giving to home mission – perhaps focusing on a specific ministry;
- Most important of all, support BRF Ministries with your prayers.

Donate at **brf.org.uk/donate** or use the form on pages 139–40.

A worldwide community of faith

Divided tongues, as of fire, appeared among them, and a tongue rested on each of them. All of them were filled with the Holy Spirit and began to speak in other languages, as the Spirit gave them ability.
ACTS 2:3–4 (NRSV)

This edition covers the period of Ascensiontide and Pentecost, a time for marvelling at the wonder of Christ ascending to heaven and the Spirit being sent down to be with us all, uniting us in Christ, beyond the boundaries of countries and languages.

Our Messy Church team is deep in the reality of this worldwide community of faith with the Messy Church Conference 2025 and Key Leaders Gathering. These events take a huge amount of planning and we are grateful to all who have been involved in making them happen.

The Anna Chaplaincy, Living Faith and Parenting for Faith teams are equally busy with training courses, attending conferences, bringing people together and equipping and resourcing people in their ministries and everyday lives.

None of this would be possible without the faith-filled generosity of our supporters. Regular giving, one-off donations, gifts in wills, grants from charitable trusts, responses to appeals and top-up donations with purchases or event bookings – every single gift helps us provide the resources that touch lives around the world. Thank you.

Find out more at **brf.org.uk/donate** or get in touch with us on **01235 462305** or via **giving@brf.org.uk**.

We thank you for your support and your prayers.

The fundraising team at BRF Ministries

> Give. Pray. Get involved.
> **brf.org.uk**

GUIDELINES SUBSCRIPTION RATES

Please note our new subscription rates, current until 30 April 2026:

Individual subscriptions
covering 3 issues for under 5 copies, payable in advance
(including postage & packing):

	UK	Europe	Rest of world
Guidelines 1-year subscription	£21.30	£29.55	£35.25

Group subscriptions
covering 3 issues for 5 copies or more, sent to one UK address (post free):

Guidelines 1-year subscription   £15.75 per set of 3 issues p.a.

Please note that the annual billing period for group subscriptions runs from 1 May to 30 April.

Overseas group subscription rates
Available on request. Please email **enquiries@brf.org.uk**.

Copies may also be obtained from Christian bookshops:

Guidelines   £5.25 per copy

All our Bible reading notes can be ordered online
by visiting **brfonline.org.uk/subscriptions**

GUIDELINES INDIVIDUAL SUBSCRIPTION FORM

To set up a recurring subscription, please go to
brfonline.org.uk/guidelines-subscription

Title .... First name/initials .... Surname ....
Address ....
.... Postcode ....
Telephone .... Email ....

Please send *Guidelines* beginning with the September 2025 / January 2026 / May 2026 issue (*delete as appropriate*):

(*please tick box*)	UK	Europe	Rest of world
Guidelines 1-year subscription	☐ £21.30	☐ £29.55	☐ £35.25

Optional donation to support the work of BRF Ministries £ ....

Total enclosed £ .... (cheques should be made payable to 'BRF')

Please complete and return the Gift Aid declaration on page 140 to make your donation even more valuable to us.

Please charge my MasterCard / Visa with £ ....

Card no. ☐☐☐☐ ☐☐☐☐ ☐☐☐☐ ☐☐☐☐

Expires end M M Y Y   Security code ☐☐☐ Last 3 digits on the reverse of the card

We will use your personal data to process this order. From time to time we may send you information about the work of BRF Ministries. Please contact us if you wish to discuss your mailing preferences **brf.org.uk/privacy**

Please return this form with the appropriate payment to:
BRF Ministries, 15 The Chambers, Vineyard, Abingdon OX14 3FE
For terms and cancellation information, please visit **brfonline.org.uk/terms**.

Bible Reading Fellowship is a charity (233280) and company limited by guarantee (301324), registered in England and Wales

BRF Ministries

Inspiring people of all ages to grow in Christian faith

BRF Ministries is the home of Anna Chaplaincy, Living Faith, Messy Church and Parenting for Faith

As a charity, our work would not be possible without fundraising and gifts in wills.
To find out more and to donate,
visit brf.org.uk/give or call +44 (0)1235 462305

Registered with FUNDRAISING REGULATOR

GUIDELINES GIFT SUBSCRIPTION FORM

☐ I would like to give a gift subscription (please provide both names and addresses):

Title _____ First name/initials _____ Surname _____

Address _____

_____ Postcode _____

Telephone _____ Email _____

Gift subscription name _____

Gift subscription address _____

_____ Postcode _____

Gift message (20 words max. or include your own gift card):

_____

_____

Please send *Guidelines* beginning with the September 2025 / January 2026 / May 2026 issue *(delete as appropriate)*:

(please tick box)	UK	Europe	Rest of world
Guidelines **1-year subscription**	☐ £21.30	☐ £29.55	☐ £35.25

Optional donation to support the work of BRF Ministries £ _____

Total enclosed £ _____ (cheques should be made payable to 'BRF')

Please complete and return the Gift Aid declaration on page 140 to make your donation even more valuable to us.

Please charge my MasterCard / Visa with £ _____

Card no. ☐☐☐☐ ☐☐☐☐ ☐☐☐☐ ☐☐☐☐

Expires end M M Y Y   Security code ☐☐☐   Last 3 digits on the reverse of the card

We will use your personal data to process this order. From time to time we may send you information about the work of BRF Ministries. Please contact us if you wish to discuss your mailing preferences **brf.org.uk/privacy**

Please return this form with the appropriate payment to:
BRF Ministries, 15 The Chambers, Vineyard, Abingdon OX14 3FE
For terms and cancellation information, please visit brfonline.org.uk/terms.

Bible Reading Fellowship is a charity (233280) and company limited by guarantee (301324), registered in England and Wales

GL0125